THE BOOKMAN'S GLOSSARY

FIFTH EDITION

THE BOOKMAN'S GLOSSARY
FIFTH EDITION

Edited by Jean Peters
Librarian, R. R. Bowker Company

R. R. BOWKER COMPANY
A Xerox Education Company
New York & London, 1975

Published by R. R. Bowker Co. (A Xerox Education Company)
1180 Avenue of the Americas, New York, N.Y. 10036
Copyright © 1975 by Xerox Corporation
All Rights reserved.
Printed and bound in the United States of America

Library of Congress Cataloging in Publication Data
Main entry under title:

The Bookman's glossary.

    1. Book industries and trade—Dictionaries.
2. Printing—Dictionaries.   3. Bibliography—
Dictionaries.   I. Peters, Jean, 1935– ed.
II. Bowker (R. R.) Company, New York.
Z118.B75 1975   010'.3   74-28432
ISBN 0-8352-0732-3

PREFACE

It has been fifty years since *The Bookman's Glossary* made its first appearance, in serial form, in the July 12, 1924, issue of *Publishers Weekly*. After appearing in installments throughout that summer, the *Glossary* was issued the following year in book form under the authorship of John A. Holden. In the half century since, it has gone through four editions, each revised and enlarged to reflect the expanding and changing terminology of the book trade. This fifth edition has been completely revised, the number of terms expanded, and the format enlarged. Its objective, like that of its predecessors, is to provide a practical guide to the terminology used in the production and distribution of books—not necessarily the technical language of the trade, but rather the words in common usage in a bookstore, in a publisher's office, in a library, or among book collectors. In this edition, the printing terminology has been broadened to include the area of computer typesetting.

The various editions of the *Glossary* have been compiled by different methods, ranging from the single authorship of the first two editions, to compilation by a committee of Bowker staff members in the third, to a single editor with subject advisors in the fourth. This fifth edition, under the direction of a general editor, has been revised by subject specialists. The terminology of the antiquarian book trade has been revised by Edward J. Lazare, former editor and publisher of *American Book Prices Current*. Paul Doebler, management consultant in printing and publishing and contributing editor to *Publishers Weekly*, revised the bookmaking terms and prepared the new definitions in the area of computer typesetting. The printing definitions have been revised by Victor Strauss, printing management consultant, and the publishing and bookselling terms, by Chandler B. Grannis, Editor-at-large, *Publishers Weekly*. The terminology in the field of library science has been revised by the editor, and the proper names revised by the editor with the help of Edward Lazare and Chandler Grannis. The subject specialists have made extensive revisions in the entries of the previous edition; they have deleted a number of terms no longer in use, and have added many new terms that have come into use in the industry in the fourteen years since the last edition.

Generally, the orientation of the book remains the same. Certain limits in the scope of the earlier editions have been retained. For example, terminology that might be used by the printer but not encountered by anyone else, has been omitted. The library science terminology has been limited to the vocabulary that would most likely be used in the publishing community—largely the terminology of research, bibliography, indexing, and to some extent, acquisitions. On the other hand, the scope of the proper names, which in previous editions had been limited to those of historic importance in the graphic arts, has been enlarged to include also those who have made a significant contribution to the world of book publishing and who have in various ways changed the industry.

The section on foreign book trade terms that appeared in the two preceding editions of the *Glossary* has been omitted from this edition. For these terms there are three separate dictionaries available from the Bowker Company: *The Publishers Practical Dictionary in 20 Languages*, edited by Dr. Imre Mora, 1974; *The Librarian's Practical Dictionary in 22 Languages*, edited by Dr. Zoltan Pipics, sixth edition, 1974; and *Manual of European Languages for Librarians*, edited by C. G. Allen, 1974. Each of these dictionaries provides far more complete coverage of the language of the foreign book trade than could be attempted by *The Bookman's Glossary*.

This edition of *The Bookman's Glossary* could not have been possible without the help of many people. The editor is especially grateful to Edward Lazare, Paul Doebler, Victor Strauss, and Chandler Grannis, all of whom gave generously of their time and knowledge to help with the revision of this edition, and also to Terry Belanger and Robert Frase for advice and assistance.

Grateful acknowledgment is made to the authors and publishers of the reference works most frequently consulted: *A New Introduction to Bibliography*, by Philip Gaskell (Oxford University Press); *Principles of Bibliographical Description*, by Fredson T. Bowers (Russell & Russell); *ABC for Book Collectors*, by John Carter (Knopf); *An Encyclopedia of the Book*, by Geoffrey Glaister (World); and other books included in the Reading List.

THE BOOKMAN'S GLOSSARY

AAs Author's alterations (*q.v.*).

AAP Association of American Publishers (*q.v.*).

AAUP Association of American University Presses (*q.v.*).

AB Abbreviation for *Antiquarian Bookman, The Weekly Magazine of the Antiquarian Booktrade*. Started by the R. R. Bowker Company and published by them from 3 January 1948 through June 1953. Since 1 July 1953, the serial has been owned and published by its editor from the start, Sol M. Malkin. It is currently issued as *AB Bookman's Weekly*. Annual numbers (*AB Bookman's Yearbook*) have been issued since 1949.

ABA American Booksellers Association (*q.v.*).

a.c.s.; a.d.s.; a.l.s.; a.ms.s.; a.n.s. Abbreviations for—autograph card, signed; autograph document, signed; autograph letter, signed; autograph manuscript, signed; and autograph note, signed. Each piece entirely in the handwriting of the signer. *See also* holograph.

ad.; advt.; advert. (British) Abbreviations for advertisement.

ALA American Library Association (*q.v.*).

AV materials *See* audiovisual materials.

access time Time taken by a computer to find the place in its memory or storage area at which data is stored or is to be stored. Two types are *read time* and *write time*. Read time is the interval required for the computer to enter data into memory; write time is the interval required to extract something from memory.

accession Addition (of books or other materials) made by a library to its collection.

added entry In cataloging, a secondary entry. Cf. main entry. Where author is used as main entry, there may be added entries for title, subjects, series, editors, translators, etc.

addenda (*sing.* **addendum**)   Brief additional data added to a book at the back, or on a separate sheet laid in. *See also* appendix; errata.

address   An identification for a specific location in the computer memory used to get back to data stored there.

adhesive binding   The fastening of pages into a book, and the cover onto a book, by means of a layer of glue along the spine. Also called *perfect binding*. In such bindings, only the glue holds the book together. On the binding machine, the folded edges of the signatures are cut off, leaving loose leaves. The binding edges of these are then roughed to form a good binding edge, and glue is applied. The cover is next applied to the glue layer. Animal glues, polyvinyl chloride glues, and hot-melt adhesives are used for this type of binding, but hot-melts are fastest-growing types in use today. Adhesive binding is used for paperbound books and also for some hardcover books. *See also* binding.

Adler, Elmer   (1884–1962)   American printer and publisher. Organized Pynson Printers, 1922. One of the founders of *The Colophon, A Book Collectors' Quarterly*; and typographical consultant to the New York *Times* and director of its Museum of the Printed Word. Later research associate in the graphic arts at Princeton University. Founder and director of La Casa del Libro, San Juan, Puerto Rico.

advance   *See* author's advance.

advance copies   Copies of a new book sent to reviewers and others before publication date. *See also* review copies.

advance on royalty   Payment to an author against expected royalties earned by the book.

advance orders   In the book industry, orders placed for books prior to publication dates; the number of orders placed far in advance, as a result of early sales efforts, often helps determine the publisher's print orders, pricing, and promotion.

advance sheets   The sheets of a book, sometimes unsewn, issued in advance of publication for review or promotion purposes.

against the grain   The direction across or against the majority of fibers in a sheet of paper. Fibers in paper tend to lie mostly in one direction, called the grain direction. Folding paper across the fibers, or against the grain, tends to weaken the sheet and produces a fold that does not stay closed as well as paper folded with the grain. In addition, when the grain runs across the page of a book, it tends to prevent the book from opening easily because the page must bend against the spring tension of the fibers. *See also* grain.

agate (1) In hand binding a piece of agate or bloodstone used in burnishing gold or colored edges. (2) The old way of designating 5½ point type, used in the advertising field to designate the amount of vertical advertising space (14 agate lines to the column inch).

agate line A standard of measurement for depth of columns of advertising space. Foureen agate lines make one *column inch.*

Aitken, Robert (1734–1802) Philadelphia printer. He printed, among many things, the first complete Bible in the English language in North America. Old Testament finished in 1782, New Testament printed in 1781. *See also* Bible in German (printed in America); and Bible in Indian (printed in America).

Aldus The shortened form of Aldus Manutius, the Latinized name of Teobaldo Manucci, or Aldo Manuzio (1450–1515), printer, publisher, critic, editor, and scholar, and the greatest of Venetian publishers. He organized his printing office in Venice in 1494, and his first publications (both in that year) were the poems of Musaeus, and the *Galeomyomachia.* These were followed in 1495 by the Latin grammar of Lascaris. Three kinds of types were designed for and used by him: roman, Greek, italic. The latter, which became known as the "Aldine Italic," first appeared in the *Virgil* of 1501. The finest of the roman fonts was used by Aldus in the only illustrated work he printed, the magnificent *Hypnerotomachia Poliphili*, which appeared in 1499.

When Aldus died in 1515, his business was continued by his father-in-law, the printer Andreas Torresanus, who died in 1529. Paulus Manutius continued the business when he came of age, and later, his son Aldus Manutius the Second took over, and with his death in 1597 the establishment came to a close.

No printer's device is better known than the device of the dolphin and anchor adapted by Aldus as his mark from a silver coin of the Emperor Vespasian. The dolphin stands for speed in execution and the anchor for firmness in deliberation. The device was later taken up by other printers, including William Pickering in the nineteenth century.

The adjective Aldine, derived from Aldus, has been applied to certain styles of display types, and to various kinds of printers' ornaments of solid face used by Aldus and other early printers. Pickering adopted the name "Aldine Poets" for his fifty-three volume edition of British Poets.

algorithm A set of rules for performing calculations, such as the procedure for computing the square root of a number. Computer programs are largely algorithmic in nature.

all firsts In cataloging, a group of first editions.

all published   A descriptive term for an uncompleted set. For example, if a publication, proposed or intended to appear in several volumes, is suspended, the fact is stated as "all published."

all rights reserved   A printed notice in a publication that any use of the book or article will not be permitted without the consent of the copyright owner. These rights include dramatic, television, broadcasting, motion picture, serial, republication, etc. Such notice is not required by copyright law, but is needed for copyright protection in certain Latin American countries, under the Buenos Aires Convention. *See also* author's rights; copyright.

allowance   In the book industry, (1) a partial payment by the publisher on advertising cost shared with the retailer; hence, "cooperative advertising"; (2) an allowance paid by the publisher on the cost of freight.

alphabet length   The length of the twenty-six letters of the alphabet in lowercase, usually stated in points. The number 341 divided by the alphabet length in points gives "characters per pica." The relative compactness of typefaces is determined by comparison of alphabet lengths.

alphanumeric   Contraction for alphabetic-numeric, indicating sets of characters, computer instructions, programs, or other elements which contain both alphabetical and numerical characters. Such character sets can also contain special symbols and punctuation as well.

alterations   Changes made in proofs.

alternative title   Subtitle introduced by "or" or its equivalent; e.g., "Twelfth Night; or, What You Will."

American Bibliography   *See* Evans, Charles.

American Book Prices Current   *See* auction prices.

American Booksellers Association   Trade association, founded in 1900, for operators of retail bookstores.

American Institute of Graphic Arts   Organized 1914 to plan U.S. participation in a Leipzig graphic arts exhibition. Has actively stimulated interest in the graphic arts and encouraged those engaged in them ever since. One of its best known events is the annual "Fifty Books of the Year" exhibit, although it now has developed programs and exhibitions for all types of graphics including magazines, television, advertising, and general printed materials.

American Library Association   Professional association of librarians and others interested in the educational, social, and cultural responsibilities of libraries. Founded in 1876.

American point system   The system adopted in 1886 by the United States Type Founders' Association, according to which the various sizes of type characters bear a fixed and simple relation one to another. It is based upon the *pica* body, and this body is divided into twelfths, or *points*, and every type body or size consists of a given number of these points. A point is .01384 inch, or very nearly ¹⁄₇₂ inch. The system is a modification of the French system. (There are different systems in some other countries, Russia, for example.)

This paragraph is set in 10-point. Commonly used text faces rarely go below 6-point or above 14-point.

Americana   Books, etc., of history, geography, travel, etc., relating (in its narrower sense) chiefly to the United States. In its broader sense, Americana relates to books, etc., concerning not only the United States, but also Canada, Mexico, Central America, South America, and the West Indies.

-ana; -iana   A suffix to names of persons or places, denoting a collection of books or other information; e.g., Americana, Johnsoniana, Lincolniana, Shaviana. The *i* is inserted for euphony.

analog computer   A computer which compares variables and indicates quantities directly by physical means, such as comparing two opposing voltages to find the difference between them. An analog computer measures quantities continuously, whereas a digital computer counts discrete units one at a time.

Anderson, Alexander (1775–1870)   First American wood engraver, notable for his illustrations in the "white-line" technique of Bewick.

annotation   A note accompanying an entry in a bibliography or catalog, intended to describe or evaluate the work cited.

annual   (1) A publication issued regularly once a year. (2) Illustrated anthologies of the nineteenth century. Many are now collected because they contain first-edition material by famous authors, often anonymous.

anonymous (anon.)   Authorship unknown or unavowed. The Copyright Office will register an anonymous work and assume that the claimant is the author or publisher.

anthology   A collection of selections from the writings of one or more authors, usually on one theme, literary type, period, nation, or the like.

antiqua   German type founding name for roman type. The common German blackface is called *fraktur* (*q.v.*).

Antiquarian Bookman   *See* AB.

antiquarian bookseller   A dealer in old, rare, and secondhand books.

Antiquarian Booksellers Association   The British trade association, founded in 1906. *See also* International League of Antiquarian Booksellers.

Antiquarian Booksellers' Association of America, Incorporated   The American trade association, founded in 1949. Address: 630 Fifth Ave., Shop 2 Concourse, New York, N.Y. 10020. *See also* International League of Antiquarian Booksellers.

antique   (1) Paper the surface of which has been neither polished (calendered) nor coated. A smooth antique is called an *eggshell* (*q.v.*). (2) Modern calf bindings made to simulate old bindings.

apocryphal   Of unknown authorship or doubtful authenticity.

appendix (*pl.* **appendixes or appendices**)   Matter which follows the text of a book. Usually material which illustrates, enlarges on, or supports by statistics the text of the volume. *Supplement* is generally more extensive matter, sometimes independent in its argument from the text or of later addition. Cf. addenda, errata.

approval plan   An agreement between a library and a publisher or dealer, under which the latter is given the responsibility of selecting and supplying all current books published in the subject areas, levels, countries, or languages specified by the library. In most approval plans, returns are permitted. *See also* blanket order.

aquatint   An intaglio process of etching on copper or steel plates to which acid-resistant granules have first been evenly adhered. Soft, water-color effects thus become possible, alone or in combination with the line effect that characterizes *etchings* (*q.v.*).

arabesque   Interlaced ornament on book covers in the style of early Arabian designers.

Arabic numerals   *See* numerals, Arabic.

area composition   As used in typesetting, the spatial positioning of type, rules, and other elements that can be set on a phototypesetting machine by means of keyboarding all the required instruction codes at a typesetting keyboard prior to actual setting of type. The photocomposing unit then exposes the type in final position on the film or paper, eliminating the need for hand cutting and pasting of individual elements after typesetting. *See also* copy block.

Armed Services Editions   Expendable paper-bound books issued by the Council on Books in Wartime from New York in 1943–47 and distributed free to members of the U.S. Armed Forces. The oblong shape, double column, of the editions was devised to make possible their printing on presses used by digests and pulp magazines. They were laid out one above the other and cut apart. The use of the books by arrangement with the copyright owners was restricted to overseas distribution and the oblong shape helped to identify them.

armorial binding A binding decorated with the arms or other device of royalty or nobility.

Arrighi, Ludovico Early sixteenth-century Roman calligrapher, type designer, and printer whose italic typefaces influenced typography in Italy and elsewhere. He is presumed to have perished in the sack of Rome in 1527.

art, artwork An overall term used to cover photographs, drawings, paintings, hand lettering, and the like, prepared to illustrate a book, pamphlet, brochure, advertisement, etc.

art paper Special heavy paper, sometimes colored, used by artists in the preparation of art work or paper constructions.

artificial language In computer science, a language based on a set of explicitly prescribed rules established before it is used to write anything. Computer programming languages such as Fortran, Cobol, Basic, etc., must be artificial languages because the machine cannot intuitively change its understanding of a natural language such as English, as it develops new dimensions. *See also* machine language; natural language.

as issued In the antiquarian trade, a descriptive term emphasizing the original format of the book.

as new A catalog description of books approaching the conditions of newness. *See also* mint.

ascender In printing, the part of a lowercase letter that extends above the size of such small letters as a, c, e, n. Examples of letters with ascenders are b, d, f, h. *See also* descender.

Ashendene Press One of the most distinguished private presses of England, founded in 1894 by C. H. St. John Hornby, partner of the bookselling firm of W. H. Smith & Son. One of the finest products of this press was an edition of Dante's works issued in 1909. The press closed its production in 1935 with *A Descriptive Bibliography*.

association books Books having autograph inscriptions or notes by the author, or books in any way intimately connected with a prominent person who may have owned or presented them.

Association of American Publishers Trade association of publishers of general, educational, trade, reference, religious, scientific, technical, and medical books. Formed by a merger in 1970 of the American Book

Publishers Council (founded 1946) and the American Educational Publishers Institute (founded 1942 as the American Textbook Publishers Institute).

Association of American University Presses Trade association, organized in 1937 after an informal beginning, for scholarly publishing divisions of colleges and universities in the United States and Canada.

asterisk (1) Star-like symbol (*) used in printing to indicate a marginal reference or footnote on the same page. (2) A series of asterisks is sometimes used to indicate an elision. (3) In the rare book trade it is sometimes used to divide several titles, in place of other punctuation.

atlas folio *See* book sizes.

auction galleries A generic term for auction houses that catalog and sell private libraries, rare books, autographs and manuscripts along with the sale of other properties (works of art, furniture, etc.). There have been, and there still are, of course, some auction houses in the United States, Canada, and Great Britain devoted solely to the sale of books and manuscripts. The best lists of firms holding book and manuscript sales are to be found in the various annual volumes of *American Book Prices Current*, in *Book Auction Records*, and in the *American Book Trade Directory* (Bowker). The best account of American book auctions is to be found in George L. McKay's *American Book Auction Catalogues, 1713–1934: A Union List* (N.Y. Public Library, 1937). This work contains a detailed historical introduction by Clarence S. Brigham, titled *The History of Book Auctions in America.*

auction prices Book sales and their prices were first regularly reported in Great Britain beginning in 1887. In the United States regular reports began in 1895. In various countries of Western Europe several series of reports were issued, some sporadically, in the twentieth century.

"Book Prices Current" began the first regular reports of sales in Great Britain and issued annual records from 1887 to 1948. Following these annual volumes, *BPC* issued two quadrennial volumes, 1949–52, and 1952–56. No further records have appeared in this series.

"Book Auction Records" began reporting sales in Great Britain in 1902. *BAR* printed the year's records in quarterly parts. Its object was to provide price records as soon as possible after the sales. This quarterly form continued through 1940. Beginning in 1941 the annual form, giving the year's entries in one alphabet, was adopted. The series is currently issued by Dawsons of Pall Mall, Folkestone, Kent, England.

"American Book Prices Current," the annual record of book and manuscript sales in the United States, was begun by Luther S. Livingston in 1895, and it has been published continuously since then. In addition to serving as editor and as editorial director of *ABPC* until his death in 1914, Livingston also edited a four-volume compilation (often miscalled a "cumulation") published in 1905, titled *Auction Prices of Books . . . A Representative Record . . . from the commencement of the English Book Prices Current in 1886 and the American Book Prices Current in 1894, to 1904; and including some thousands of important auction quotations of earlier date.* The *ABPC* is currently issued by American Book Prices Current, 121 E. 78 St., New York, N.Y. 10021.

Book and manuscript sales in the United States from 1941 through 1951 were also reported in *United States Cumulative Book Auction Records.* This publication ceased with the 1951 annual.

Book auction sales in France from October 1918 to July 1931 were reported in *Annuaire des Ventes de Livres*, edited by Leo Delteil, and published in 12 volumes, Paris, 1920–1931. Further French sales were recorded after World War II, when *Le Guide du Bibliophile et du Libraire*, edited by Eric de Grolier, appeared in 1946; this series, in five volumes, covered the sales held in 1944, 1945, 1946–48, 1949–51, and 1952–56. Under different titles and by various publishers, French book auction records have been continued from 1964 through 1972.

Book auction sales in Western Germany, Holland, Austria, and Switzerland have been reported annually since 1950 in *Jahrbuch der Auktionspreise*, published by Dr. Ernst Hauswedell & Co., in Hamburg, Germany.

audiovisual materials (1) Generally, supplementary teaching materials used in the classroom, library, and the like. Materials usually considered audiovisual include charts, graphs, maps, pictures, slides, filmstrips, recordings, tapes, motion pictures, television, programmed learning aids, objects, specimens, and models. (2) More specifically, and by extension, nonbook materials, such as tapes, slides, and filmstrips, which require the use of special equipment in order to be seen or heard.

author The original writer or composer of a book, treatise, or document, as distinguished from an editor, compiler, or translator. The term "author" under the U.S. Copyright Law includes employers in cases where the work is done for hire. *See also* joint author; royalties.

author earn-out The sales income figure at which the amount given the author in advance payment is earned back.

author entry Entry of a work, in a catalog or index, under the name of its author; usually the main entry (*q.v.*).

author-publisher A writer who is his own publisher. *See also* privately printed.

author-title index   In a bibliography, an index that enters each book by title as well as by the author's name, either in two alphabets, or combined in one alphabet.

author's advance   Payment or payments made by a publisher to an author prior to completion and delivery of final manuscript; usually specified during negotiation of a contract between author and publisher.

author's agent   *See* literary agent.

author's alterations (AAs)   Changes to typeset matter made by the author, apart from those necessary to correct printer's errors. Alterations are billed as a separate item by the typesetter, and it is customary for the publisher to pass on to the author some part of the charge—often the amount by which the alterations exceed 5 to 10 percent of the basic composition bill. *See also* misprint.

author's copies   The complimentary copies, usually six or more, of his book given to the author by the publisher.

author's proof   The proof sent to the author for his OK or correction.

author's rights   Under the U.S. Copyright Act the author of a copyrighted work has the right to print, publish, copy and sell; to translate or make any other version; to dramatize. The author of a drama has the right to convert it into a nondramatic work, to perform publicly, to record. The author of a lecture, sermon, address or other nondramatic literary work has, in addition to the basic rights mentioned above, the right to deliver publicly for profit or authorize delivery.

These rights may be assigned under contract separately or together. The term *author* includes employer in the case of works made for hire, as a map, motion picture or encyclopedia. *See also* copyright.

autograph   (1) In the rare book trade, letters, documents, cards, etc., written or signed with a person's own hand *See also* the abbreviations *a.c.s.*; *a.d.s.*; *a.l.s.*; etc. (2) In the new book trade, an "autographing party" is a publicity device whereby an author signs copies of his book for customers in a bookshop.

automatic data processing   The computation, sorting, merging, or otherwise handling of data by means of electronic or electrical machinery which operates with a minimum of human intervention.

automatic distribution   A procedure in which a publisher supplies books for stock to a bookstore according to the publisher's determination of approximate quantities. In trade publishing, quantities are usually subject to the dealer's acceptance. Fully automated distribution is customary in the mass market paperback industry.

autopositive A type of photographic material which will produce a direct copy of a subject without first making a separate negative.

auxiliary storage A storage or memory device outside of the main memory in the computer itself. Auxiliary devices include magnetic tape, disk or drum units, and usually hold much larger amounts of data although access time to the data usually is slower.

avant garde French: vanguard. Used as noun and adjective to characterize the expression by individuals and literary groups of experimental or unorthodox forms, ideas, and theories, usually addressed to a limited audience. Often applied to "little" magazines, free verse, experimental fiction, new philosophical, literary, artistic, or political-social ideas, especially in the forty-odd years from about 1920.

BAL *See* Bibliography of American Literature.

bds. Abbreviation for *boards* (*q.v.*).

bf Abbreviation for *boldface* (*q.v.*).

BIP Abbreviation for *Books in Print*, the annual author-title index of books in print and for sale in the United States. Published by the R.R. Bowker Company.

BMI *See* Book Manufacturers' Institute.

b.o. Abbreviation for "back order."

back margin *See* margins.

back matter Also called: reference matter; appendix; addenda; author's notes; glossary; bibliography; index.

back order An unfilled order held for future delivery.

back strip A strip of paper, cloth, or other material pasted to the back of the folded sheets in the binding of a book. In the antiquarian trade the term is also used to mean the outer spine of a bound book.

back up (1) To print the reverse of a sheet already printed on one side. *See also* work and turn. (2) In computer technology a backup machine will accept the same data and programs as the primary unit in case the first one should break down. Backup units may be in the same plant or office, or they may be available over transmission lines.

backbone The back of a bound book, connecting the two covers. Also called *spine, shelfback.*

backed (1) In bookbinding, a book that has passed through the backing step. (2) Description of a leaf, for example a frontispiece, which has been repaired by mounting upon, or being backed by, a new leaf. When highly transparent silk is applied to both sides, the leaf is described as *silked*.

backing   The process of gluing the rounded back of a book and applying reinforcing liner and/or crash. Backing follows the rounding operation and precedes casing-in.

backlining   *See* lining.

backlist   The titles on a publisher's list which are older than the current season.

bad break   (1) In page makeup, an illogical or aesthetically displeasing beginning or end of a type column, such as a one- or two-word paragraph ending at the top or a subheading occurring on the last line. Always avoided in careful work. (2) In computer typesetting, an improper word division and hyphenation decision made by a computer while following an automatic hyphenation program. *See also* hyphenation.

bands   (1) The horizontal cords running across the spine of a book to which the signatures of the book are sewed. (2) The ridges across the spine of a bound book, under which are the cords.

banned   Prohibited from sale by ecclesiastical or secular authority. *See also* censor; censorship.

basic weight   *See* basis weight.

basis weight   The weight of a ream (500 sheets) of paper of a basic size. All papers are classified into certain categories — such as book papers, bonds, bristols, cover stocks—and each category has a basic size which is used as a standard in expressing weight. The basis weight is always stated in terms of the basic size, even though the actual sheets may be cut to a different size.

The basic size for all book papers is 25 × 38 inches. Therefore, a "60 pound book paper" would be one for which 500 sheets cut to 25 × 38 inches in size would weigh 60 pounds. The fact that the actual sheets to be used might be a different size would not affect the paper's designation as a 60 pound sheet.

Baskerville, John   (1706–1775)   English printer and type founder of the eighteenth century. In turn stone-cutter, writing master, and manufacturer of japanned ware, he turned his attention about 1750 to type designing and printing, and in 1758 was elected printer to the University of Cambridge. His first work was an edition of Virgil (1757). Dedicated to excellence in all elements of book design and production, he did much to raise and influence the standards of his day.

bastard title   The title of a book standing by itself on a page preceding the full title page. Now often also referred to as *half title* (*q.v.*).

batch processing   Processing data or programs in sequence in the order received or submitted; first in, first out; last in, last out.

battered   In letterpress, type matter or other printing surfaces so worn or injured that they give defective impressions.

battledore   A child's lesson sheet, especially one made of a wooden tablet or varnished cardboard. In use in the late eighteenth century superseding the *hornbook* (*q.v.*).

Bay Psalm Book   The familiar designation for *The Whole Booke of Psalmes*, the first book of size printed in what is now the United States, and called the *Bay Psalm Book* from its origin in Massachusetts Bay Colony. It was also known at various times as the *New England Psalm Book*, and as the *New England Version of the Psalms*. It is the earliest work printed in the United States known to be extant. It was printed in 1640, by Stephen Daye (or Day), at Cambridge, Massachusetts.

bearers   (1) Type-high strips of metal arranged around pages of type when they are locked in forms from which electrotype plates are to be made. (2) In lithographic presses, bearers are rings of steel attached to both ends of cylinders, providing rolling contact and serving as surfaces of reference in the making of certain adjustments.

bed   Surface of printing press, against which type is clamped.

Beirut Agreement   (Agreement for Facilitating the International Circulation of Visual and Auditory Materials of an Educational, Scientific, and Cultural Character) A UNESCO-sponsored international agreement which removes tariffs, discriminatory taxation, quotas, and exchange restrictions for the importation of audiovisual materials certified by the countries of exportation as being of an educational, scientific, or cultural character. Drafted in 1948, the agreement was ratified by the United States in 1967; by 1973 there were twenty-eight countries as members. A conference was called in Geneva in 1973 to review the Beirut Agreement and the related Florence Agreement (*q.v.*).

Bell, John (1745–1831)   English bookseller, printer, publisher, type founder, and journalist. Responsible for many innovations in printing—the first to use modern face in England, the first to abolish the long ſ in printing and the first to adapt the high standards of Baskerville and Bodoni to the making of low-priced books.

belles lettres   Polite or elegant literature; this term is now applied somewhat vaguely to literary works in which imagination and taste are predominant.

belt press   A rotary web letterpress for producing a complete book in one pass of the paper through the machine. It is equipped with two endless plastic belts, one for printing each side of the paper. The printing plates, either rubber or plastic, are mounted on these variable-length belts. The press has two printing stations, one for each belt and each side of the paper. After the first side is printed, the paper is turned and put through the second printing station. After printing, the web of paper is slit, folded, cut into page lengths and finally collated into a complete book. Books are then fed into an adhesive binder, often automatically, as they come out of the press. It is possible to produce a bound book from blank paper with the belt press within approximately two minutes. The machine eliminates the traditional printing of books in sections or signatures, one at a time, and the subsequent folding and gathering operations. This greatly reduces the handling required in the plant and the time needed to produce a printing. The first successful belt press, the Cameron Book Production System, was installed in 1968 by Cameron Machine Co., Dover, N.J., at Kingsport Press, Kingsport, Tenn.

Benday (Ben Day) process (1) The process invented by Benjamin Day, a New York printer (1838–1916), for mechanically producing a great variety of shaded tints and mottled effects on line or halftone printing plates. (2) Mechanical screens and patterns applied by the artist to the original art work in the form of transparent printed overlays, rather than by the photoengraver or lithographer to the printing plate.

Bensley, Thomas (1785–1833) Distinguished London printer. Promoter in England of the power-driven press.

Berne Convention Common name for the agreement establishing the International Union for the Protection of Literary and Artistic Works, to which more than sixty nations are signatory. Begun in Berne, Switzerland, in 1866, and revised four times: Paris, 1896; Berlin, 1908; Rome, 1928; Brussels, 1948. The latest general revision, signed at Stockholm on July 14, 1967, will come into effect when five countries have ratified or acceded to it. Protection under these conventions is extended without formalities to works by nationals of any country on the sole condition that first publication take place in a country that belongs to the Berne Union. The United States is not a member, but, under this proviso, American works can achieve protection in Union countries by simultaneous publication in a member country, such as Great Britain or Canada. With other non-Union countries, the United States has agreements and proclamations of varying character to protect literary property, and is a signatory of the more recent *Universal Copyright Convention (q.v.).* Both the Berne and the Universal Copyright Conventions underwent additional revisions in 1971 at Paris, specifically in order to ease developing countries' access to translation and reproduction rights to educational and cultural materials.

best sellers   Books in most active current demand. Frequently quoted lists of best sellers in the bookstores are compiled weekly by the New York *Times*, *Time* magazine, and other consumer publications, and by *Publishers Weekly*. Other lists report the best-selling books in specific categories (e.g., religious books, mass market paperbacks) or in a publisher's own list.

beveled boards   Bookbinder's boards given a slanting or beveled edge before the covering material is put on. A feature of custom-bound leather bindings on extra-heavy volumes.

Bewick, Thomas (1753–1828)   *See* woodcut.

bibelot   A small decorative article of virtu that is rare, curious, or beautiful. The word is used by some book catalogers to describe a small decorative book or literary trinket.

Bible in English (1782, 1781, printed in America)   *See* Aitken, Robert.

Bible in German (1743, printed in America)   *See* Sauer, Christopher.

Bible in Indian (Massachusetts, 1663, 1661, the first Bible printed in America)   *See* Eliot, John.

Bible paper   A thin but opaque book paper, possessing strength and durability; suitable for Bibles, encyclopedias, catalogs, etc., where reduction in bulk is desirable. *See also* India paper; Oxford India paper.

Biblia Pauperum (Bible of the poor)   The best known of the *block books* (*q.v.*), consisting almost entirely of pictures, with text forming an integral part of the picture page. The pictures and the explanatory text (intended to teach Biblical truths) were printed from wooden blocks on which the pictures and text were cut by hand. The earlier examples were printed on one side of the leaf only. About ten separate editions in the block book form are known to have been issued, beginning in about 1450, some in Latin and some in German. They were not superseded by the invention of printing with movable metal type, but were produced alongside the early printed books until the early sixteenth century. Although printed in large numbers, the block book form of the *Biblia Pauperum* is today of extreme rarity; only fifteen copies are known to be in existence. An edition printed from metal type was issued in about 1462 by Albrecht Pfister of Bamberg.

biblio   A combining form from Greek "biblion," *book*. Some examples are: *biblioclast*, a destroyer or mutilator of books; *biblioklept*, one who steals books; *bibliomancy*, divination by books, especially by passages of Scripture taken at random; *bibliomania*, a mania for acquiring books; *bibliopegy*, the art of binding books; *bibliophile*, a lover of books; *bibliopole*, a bookseller; *bibliotaph*, one who hides away books, as in a tomb; *bibliotheca*, a library.

bibliographic information interchange format "A format for the exchange, rather than the local processing, of bibliographic records."*

bibliography (1) The art or science of the description and history of books (their physical makeup, authorship, editions, printing, publication, etc.). (2) Loosely, the science of books; bibliology. (3) A list of works on a given subject or by a given author; the literature of a subject.

Bibliography of American Literature Compiled by Jacob Blanck, published by Yale University Press, 1955– .

A definitive bibliography of American literature of the past 150 years. When completed the work will contain some 35,000 items by nearly 300 selected authors, from the beginning of the Federal period up to and including authors who died before the end of 1930. The emphasis is on authors of *belles lettres* or work of like character; historians and writers of travel books are included only if of literary interest. Authors primarily of juvenile literature, of scientific and medical works, textbooks, sermons, or similar material are excluded. It is planned to have the work completed in eight or nine volumes.

Six volumes have been published to date: (I) Henry Adams to Donn Byrne, 1955; (II) G. W. Cable to Timothy Dwight, 1957; (III) Edward Eggleston to Bret Harte, 1959; (IV) Nathaniel Hawthorne to Joseph Holt Ingraham, 1963; (V) Washington Irving to Henry W. Longfellow, 1969; (VI) Augustus B. Longstreet to Thomas W. Parsons, 1973.

Bibliotheca Americana *See* Sabin, Joseph.

bimetallic plates For very long runs in offset lithography, bimetallic plates of different makes may be used. The printing areas are usually copper, the nonprinting ones are of another metal, such as nickel or chromium, for example.

binary A situation in which there can be only two possible conditions. The binary number system, which is the basis of digital computers, uses only the digits zero and one. In a computer, the presence of an electrical pulse represents a one, the absence of a pulse represents a zero.

binder (1) One who binds books. (2) A detachable cover for filing magazines, pamphlets, loose-leaf sheets, etc.

binder's board A stiff, high-grade composition board used in bookbinding underneath the cloth, more dense than *chip board* (*q.v.*).

---

*This material is reproduced with permission from American National Standard Bibliographic Information Interchange on Magnetic Tape, Z39.2 copyright 1971 by the American National Standards Institute, copies of which may be purchased from the American National Standards Institute at 1430 Broadway, New York, N.Y. 10018.

binder's dies   Designs or lettering cut or etched in brass or other hard metal and used in stamping or embossing book covers. Sometimes called *binder's stamps* or *book-stamp*.

binding   (1) The structural materials such as thread and glue holding a book together, plus the attached cover of a book or pamphlet which may be cloth, leather, boards, paper, or other material. (2) In book manufacturing, the process of assembling the finished book, which includes folding, gathering, collating, sewing, tipping, gluing off, trimming, rounding and backing, lining up, casing-in, and finally, jacketing.

Edition binding is the term used for binding books in hard covers, in commercial quantities; also called *trade binding* or *publisher's binding. Hand* or *custom binding* is the binding process carried out as a hand craft. *Library bindings* are specially reinforced for library use. When this is done to sheets before the book has been given a trade binding, it is known as *prebinding.* When it is done after the book has been bound, whether before or after library use, it is known as *rebinding.* Mechanical binding uses plastic or metal material to bind the pages; various types of mechanical binding include *loose-leaf, plastic comb,* and *spiral wire binding. Pamphlet binding* is the binding of self-covered or paper-covered booklets. *Adhesive binding* is a glued binding such as that used on large telephone books and many paperback books; also called *perfect binding.*

Full binding denotes a book bound entirely in leather. *Three-quarter binding* is a binding with a leather back and leather corners. The leather of the back and that of the corners almost meet. There are no exact standards, since this is a matter of graceful proportion. *Half-binding* is similar to three-quarter binding except that a small proportion of leather is used. *Quarter-binding* is a binding with a leather back only. Often described as boards (or cloth), leather back.

binding cloth   *See* book cloth.

Binny and Ronaldson   Archibald Binny and James Ronaldson established, in Philadelphia in 1796, the first type foundry in the United States to achieve permanency. The firm published in 1812 the earliest known American type specimen book.

bit   Abbreviation for binary digit. The word can be used to mean a single unit (one or zero) in a binary number, an electrical pulse or group of pulses, or a unit of data storage capacity in a memory device.

black and white print   Any printed image using only blacks or gray tones on a white base sheet. It can refer to photographic prints as well as ink on paper prints.

black-letter   A term applied to the book-hand and types derived therefrom which developed north of the Alps—boldfaced and angular—from which is descended the modern German fraktur. Black-letter, now known to modern printers as Old English (*q.v.*), or Elizabethan, was a name invented in the seventeenth century for the types imitated from the handwriting current in England two centuries previously. It was a great contrast to types founded on the Roman or Italian hand revived by scholars of the Renaissance. Also called *gothic*. *See also* roman.

blackface   *See* boldface.

Blaeu, Willem Janszoon (1571–1638)   Founder of the Dutch printing and publishing house of Blaeu, makers of maps, atlases, and globes. He was at one time associated with Tycho Brahe, the famous Danish astronomer. Blaeu is credited with the first significant improvements in the printing press since the days of Gutenberg. The business was carried on and extended by his son John and grandson Willem. Their "Novus Atlas" in six large folio volumes was issued in 1676.

Blake, William (1757–1827)   English artist, author, poet, printer, and engraver. Experimented with etched plates on which both text and illustration were printed by a method he devised. He and his wife colored many of the illustrations by hand.

blank   An unprinted leaf which is part of a signature (*q.v.*).

blanket order   An agreement between a library and a publisher or dealer wherein the library will automatically receive one copy of each title of a publisher's output, or one copy of each title in selected subject categories. In most blanket order plans, return privileges are not permitted. Also known as a *gathering plan*. A variation on the blanket order plan is the *approval plan* (*q.v.*) in which returns are usually permitted.

   The blanket order plan, which largely replaces book selection work done within the library, is usually practiced by the larger public and academic libraries, and has the advantages of: (1) getting new publications into the library as close to publication date as possible; (2) reducing paper work; and (3) cutting acquisitions costs.

   Although there are a number of variations on the blanket order plan, one of the oldest and best known is the Greenaway Plan, named for its originator in 1958, Emerson Greenaway, for many years Director of the Free Library of Philadelphia. Under the Greenaway Plan, publishers send all their trade books to a library before publication, at the same time review copies are sent out. The plan is used chiefly by public libraries where there is a special need to buy multiple copies of books and to get them to the readers as fast as possible.

blanking In binding, the polished impression on cloth covers made with a heated brass stamp as a base for lettering or decorative stamping.

bleed (1) In layout, extending of a printed image (picture, tint block, etc.) to the very edge of the page, so that no unprinted margin shows. Depending on how many edges a picture or color block touches, pages can bleed one, two, three, or four sides. (2) In lithographic and other chemical printing, a defect due to unwanted dissolving of ink pigment, which results in a stain, or slight change in color, or fuzziness of color image.

blending Term sometimes used as a synonym for merging when referring to tape handling. *See also* merging.

blind keyboard A keyboard-equipped device for encoding data into machine-readable form, but which lacks any device for producing a typescript or hard copy as material is typed. *See also* hard copy.

blind tooling or stamping Impressions on the cover of a book made by tools or dies without the use of color or metal foil. Also called *blind blocking*.

block (1) To mount a *cut* (*q.v.*) on a block of wood or metal to make it type-high. Also British term for a cut. (2) In a computer, a group of computer words stored in successive memory locations, or handled in the machine as a unit. *See also* word.

block books (or xylographica) In the early years of the fifteenth century, woodcuts and engravings of religious subjects became well known in Northern Europe. As early as 1418 and 1423 woodcuts were made containing dated inscriptions cut on the blocks. As the difference between cutting a few words on a wood block and cutting a text upon it was slight, the next logical step was to cut upon sets of blocks not only illustrations but also text, and to bind the impressions from these blocks into volumes. The books so made are termed *block books*, and are looked upon as the intermediate step between the isolated woodcut and books printed from movable type. However, the more popular of the block books continued to be issued for more than half a century after the invention of printing with movable type.

Among the best known block books are the *Biblia Pauperum* (*q.v.*); the *Apocalypse of St. John;* the *Canticum Canticorum*; *the Ars Memorandi* (*How to Remember the Evangelists*); the popular *Ars Moriendi* (*Art of Dying*); and the *Speculum Humanae Salvationis* (*Mirror of Human Salvation*). Despite the large printings of many of the titles, block books today are of extreme rarity.

block printing Printing from hand-carved wood or linoleum blocks. *See also* block books.

blocking   Stamping (*q.v.*).

blowup   An enlargement of a photograph, jacket, sample page of a book, review, etc., used for advertising display.

blueprint   A same-size copy from a translucent original often used for showing proofs from offset negatives prior to making offset plates. The original, together with sensitized blueprint paper, is exposed to strong light. The resultant print is blue except where shielded by ink on the original.

   The word is used loosely to cover other so-called "whiteprint" processes (Ozalid, Bruning) which produce same-size copies from translucent originals. These other processes, technically the Diazo processes, are more dimensionally stable, and produce a positive from a positive in black or brown or even other colors, as well as blue. A vandyke is a brown blueprint. *See also* proofs.

blurb   The publisher's "selling talk" used on the jacket of a book or in an advertisement of it. Coined by Gelett Burgess in 1907 as a descriptive term for puffing one's own wares.

boards   The stiff boards used for the sides of books. Made of reclaimed and reprocessed waste paper, boards may be covered with paper, cloth, leather, or other material. A book is said to be bound in "boards" when the boards are covered with paper only.

Bodoni, Giambattista (1740–1813)   A world famous printer of Parma, who designed the first modern face roman types. His influence has been felt in the printing of all countries. His types, and those that developed from them, became known as modern, and the Caslon and Dutch types, which came back to popularity in the middle of the nineteenth century, as old style. These terms still persist. His two-volume *Manuale Typografico*, a catalog of his typefaces, was published in 1818.

body   (1) In metal type, a rectangular piece of metal having a raised type image on one end. The term has been carried over into photographic and struck-image typesetting to express the total vertical dimension within which the type character is located. Thus a 7 pt. typeface may be set on an 8 pt. or a 9 pt. body. This is usually expressed as setting type "7 on 8" or "7 on 9." (2) In bookbinding, the main block of pages which is bound together and then fastened to the covers.

body type   Type used in text matter as opposed to headings and display type.

boldface   Heavy-faced type, also called *blackface*, in contradistinction to *lightface*.

bolt   The folded or doubled edge of paper at the head, foot, or fore-edge of an untrimmed book.

book   "A non-periodical literary publication containing 49 or more pages, not counting covers" (UNESCO recommendation adopted in 1964). A slight variation appears in ANSI Standard Z-39.8, also used by the U.S. Bureau of the Census, which includes as books publications of less than forty-nine pages provided they have hard covers.

In U.S. Postal Service regulations, a book in order to qualify for the uniform, nationwide "special fourth class rate" (originally the "book rate" and then "the educational materials rate") must be a publication of twenty-four or more pages, at least twenty-two of which are printed, consisting wholly of reading matter or scholarly bibliography, and containing no advertising matter other than incidental announcements of books, which cannot be mailed in parcels exceeding seventy pounds in weight. Also continuing in force is a special "library rate" for the mailing of books and other materials between libraries and their patrons. Full details and definitions are contained in the *Postal Manual*, a continuing publication of the U.S. Postal Service.

Less formally, a book may be any collection of pages or leaves of any material, bound or sometimes unbound, in manuscript or in reproduction, in the form of a scroll (*q.v.*) or codex (*q.v.*); or it may be inscribed in stone or clay or appear in a variety of other forms. In the magazine industry, a specific magazine or issue of a magazine is often referred to as "the book."

Book Auction Records   *See* auction prices.

book cloth   Specially prepared cloth material used to make covers for books. Cotton gray goods, woven as for any other fabric, are used as the base material for book cloth which falls into three main categories: starch-filled, plastic-impregnated, and plastic coated (or imitation leather). The same gray goods can be finished in any of the three ways. Gray goods come in several different weights and weaves. The quality of the gray goods is based on the number of threads per square inch and the tensile strength of the threads. Book cloth comes in standard width rolls of 36, 38, 40, and 42 inches, and of varying lengths from 60 to 200 yards. For library binders, smaller rolls are available. Starch-filled cloth was the earliest form of book cloth. Today it is used on all types of books except textbooks. Plastic (originally pyroxylin, later vinyl) impregnated book cloth may be required by state specifications for textbooks. Coated book cloth is used where the effect of a leather binding is desired.

Book cloth is generally further classified as follows:

Linens—Cloth which is not dyed before the filling and color are put on.

This gives a two-tone effect because of the white threads which show through filling. Both starch-filled and plastic.

Solid or vellum—This means a smooth finish and a solid color. The cloth is dyed first and then coated, and when the cloth is finished, even though the weave of the cloth shows slightly, the color is evenly distributed over the cloth. This finish may be had on starch-filled or plastic impregnated cloth.

Natural finish—Cloth that is dyed, then filled entirely from the wrong side. In the finishing process the face side remains soft and slightly fuzzy.

Buckrams—There are several different weights of buckram but all can be identified by the heavy, coarse threads. Some buckrams are so tightly woven with such heavy threads that they are really canvas. Buckrams can be made in both linen and vellum solid color finish, and either starch-filled or plastic impregnated.

Plastic coated material cannot be made in linen finish as the main idea of this is to hide as completely as possible the fact that there is a cloth base for the material. It is made in two-tone materials, however, one of the most common being the widely used Spanish (antique) finish.

The first commercial use of cloth for bookbinding was made by William Pickering of London about 1820. Previous to that time, publishers issued their books in paper-covered wooden boards, paper-covered cardboards, vellum, wrappers, or leather. John Carter's *Binding Variants in English Publishing, 1820–1900, More Binding Variants*, and *Publisher's Cloth* give interesting historical information.

book club (1) A business that sells books by mail under a subscription agreement. A "member" (subscriber) of a book club usually receives a relatively expensive book premium for "joining" (subscribing) and agrees (though not in all clubs) to purchase some minimum number of books per year. Selections offered by clubs may be books especially reprinted for club distribution, or purchased by the club from the publisher's stock, or produced as fine original editions for subscribers only. The oldest general-interest book clubs are the Book-of-the-Month Club (1926) and the Literary Guild (1927). There are scores of special-interest book club plans offering volumes in the arts, professions, business, recreational areas, and other categories. (2) A private, noncommercial club of book collectors and bibliophiles. *See also* book-collectors' clubs. (3) A group of readers, sometimes called *reading circle* (*q.v.*), who buy books for circulation and possibly discussion among themselves (especially in Europe).

book collector One who puts purpose and system into the acquisition of books. The purpose may be general, as expressing a desire to have a useful and enjoyable library, or it may be specific with the intention of covering one or more special areas of interest, or it may be to satisfy the taste of a connoisseur or the researches of a scholar.

book-collectors' clubs   In the English-speaking world the oldest and most exclusive book-collectors' club is the Roxburghe Club, of London, founded shortly after the sale by auction of the library of the Duke of Roxburghe in 1812. The many other clubs, most of them in the United States, were founded in the past ninety years.

The oldest existing American club, the Grolier Club of New York, was founded in 1884. The objects of all of the clubs were similar to that set forth in the constitution of the Grolier: ". . . the literary study and promotion of the arts pertaining to the production of books, including the occasional publication of books designed to illustrate, promote and encourage those arts. . ." etc. The Grolier was followed shortly by:

Club of Odd Volumes (Boston, 1886)
Rowfant Club (Cleveland, 1892)
Philobiblon Club (Philadelphia, 1893)
Caxton Club (Chicago, 1895)
Dibdin Club (New York, 1897)

More followed in the twentieth century: The Franklin Club of St. Louis; the Carteret Club of Newark; the Book Club of California; the Zamorano Club of Los Angeles; etc.

The Hroswitha Club, a club of women book collectors, bibliographers, and others interested in the arts of the book, was founded in 1944 in New York. The club was named for Hroswitha, the Saxon nun of the tenth century, who was a dramatist and poet (and probably a book collector), canoness of the Abbey of Gandersheim, Saxony.

book end   A right-angled device, or solid block, generally of metal or wood, intended to hold in place a row of books.

book fair   (1) An exhibition of books and related materials, along with talks by authors and illustrators, and other events. (2) A trading center for the sale of books and rights and the making of publishing and co-publishing arrangements, or for the presentation of books available for sale or resale. Book trading fairs are now held in several countries of both hemispheres. The fairs began in the early sixteenth century in Frankfurt, Germany, and to this day, the major international one is the annual Frankfurt Book Fair. (3) Antiquarian Booksellers' Associations of different countries now also hold fairs in various cities of Europe and North America, and, in 1972, Tokyo, Japan was host to the ILAB (*q.v.*).

Book of Hours; Horae; Livre d'Heures   Book of devotions (*Hours* of the Virgin Mary, passages from the Gospels, private prayers, etc.) intended for the use of clergy and laymen. In general use in the Catholic Church from the fourteenth to the sixteenth centuries. The manuscript copies, written on vellum, were in many cases brilliantly illustrated and illuminated in colors, and they were costly. The invention of printing made possible the production of inexpensive copies and brought them within the reach of a wider public. The first printed *Livre d'Heures* was issued by Antoine Verard in Paris in 1487. The finest editions were produced in Paris between 1490 and 1505, by Pierre Pigouchet, who printed mainly for the publisher Simon Vostre, and by Thielman Kerver. Various editions were brought out until 1568, after which date publication ceased when Pope Pius V decreed that it need no longer be used by the clergy.

Book of Kells   *See* Kells.

Book Manufacturers' Institute (BMI)   Trade association of book manufacturers and book-materials suppliers. Founded in 1920.

book paper   A general term to indicate a class of printing paper used for books, periodicals, catalogs, and other job printing, as distinct from newsprint, for example.

book post; book rate   *See* book.

Book Prices Current   *See* auction prices.

book scout   A person who travels about the country, visiting book and antique shops and the like, buying items which he believes are desired by dealers, librarians, and collectors, and which he can turn over at a profit.

book sizes   There is much confusion about the definition of book sizes and little consistency in usage. The common book trade designation of sizes was based originally on the relation to a sheet of paper measuring approximately 19 × 25 inches. When folded once to make two leaves (four pages), it was a folio; when folded twice, to make four leaves (eight pages), it was a quarto; when folded to eight leaves (sixteen pages), an octavo; when folded to sixteen leaves (thirty-two pages), a sixteenmo, etc. This is the historical background of book sizes and is still used in the rare book trade. In exact bibliographical descriptions, as in describing rare books, the historical definition applies.

However, present trade practice almost invariably refers to a measurement of the height of the binding, not the size of the leaf. Usual library practice calls for the use of centimeters, the measurement again referring to the height of the binding.

With the present variety of paper sizes all dimensions are approximate:

F—folio, F°, over 30 cm. (approx. 15 in.) high.
Q—quarto, 4to, 30 cm. (approx. 12 in.) high.
O—octavo, 8vo, 25 cm. (approx. 9¾ in.) high.

D—duodecimo, 12mo, 20 cm. (approx. 7¾ in.) high.
S—sixteenmo, 16mo, 17½ cm. (approx. 6¾ in.) high.
T—twentyfourmo, 24mo, 15 cm. (approx. 5¾ in.) high.

Other sizes include:

Double elephant folio, approx. 50 in. high.
Atlas folio, approx. 25 in. high.
Elephant folio, approx. 23 in. high.
Thirtytwomo, 32mo, approx. 5 in. high.
Fortyeightmo, 48mo, approx. 4 in. high.
Sixtyfourmo, 64mo, approx. 3 in. high.

Any book which is wider than it is high is designated as oblong and such descriptive note is abbreviated obl. or ob. and precedes such terms as quarto, octavo, etc. If the book is unusually narrow for its height, it is designated narrow and such descriptive note is abbreviated nar.

English usage is even more detailed than American, and includes the following:

	Height		*Width*
Pott Octavo	6¼	×	4 inches
Foolscap Octavo	6¾	×	4¼
Crown Octavo	7½	×	5
Large Post Octavo	8¼	×	5¼
Demy Octavo	8¾	×	5⅝
Medium Octavo	9	×	5¾
Royal Octavo	10	×	6¼
Super Royal Octavo	10	×	6¾
Imperial Octavo	11	×	7½
Foolscap Quarto	8½	×	6¾
Crown Quarto	10	×	7½
Large Post Quarto	10½	×	8¼
Demy Quarto	11¼	×	8¾
Medium Quarto	11½	×	9
Royal Quarto	12½	×	10
Foolscap Folio	13½	×	8½

book-stamp   *See* binder's dies.

Book Token   A gift certificate (*q.v.*) used in the British retail book trade. U.S. version promoted by the American Booksellers Association is the Give-a-Book Certificate.

book trade   (1) Retail bookselling as a whole, considered with its practices, codes, relations with publishers and wholesalers, etc. (2) Loosely, the general, especially trade book, business.

book traveler   A publisher's salesman. *See also* traveler.

Book Week   A week designated by some group or organization for a cooperative promotion of books and reading. It may be dedicated to the promotion of libraries and reading in general as National Library Week, to national book interest, as Canadian Book Week, to local promotion, as Melbourne Book Week, to a special type of book, as Catholic Book Week or National Bible Week, or to enlist wider support for a public library. The American Merchant Marine Library has an annual drive for books for merchant seamen which is also called Book Week.

In the United States, usually a contraction for Children's Book Week, a special book promotion event held annually since 1919, usually in early November. It is sponsored by the Children's Book Council, which provides posters and other promotional material for the cooperating schools, bookstores, and libraries. Several countries hold simultaneous Book Weeks. In England such Book Weeks are held in the children's rooms of various libraries under the sponsorship of the National Book League.

booklet   A small book or pamphlet, usually paperbound.

bookmobile   (1) An automobile or "book truck" arranged for the display and distribution of books sent out by public libraries to city neighborhoods or rural areas. (2) A bookshop on wheels to bring books to small communities. (3) A traveling display of books sent out by publishers and jobbers to dealers, schools and libraries.

bookplate   A label placed in a book for identification of ownership. Bookplates of famous people or collections enhance the value of volumes. Bookplates are collected for artistic, association or historic interest and there is a large literature on the subject.

The use of bookplates is of some antiquity, and mention has been made of one dated in the middle of the fifteenth century, but at present the fine bookplates of Bilibaldus Pirckheimer (1470–1530), designed by Albrecht Dürer, are the earliest plates of high repute. Engraved English bookplates are not found of so early a date, but an old folio volume from Henry VIII's library, now in the British Museum, contains an elaborately emblazoned drawing which formed the bookplate of Cardinal Woolsey, with his arms, supporters, and cardinal's hat.

bookworm   (1) The larva of an insect, probably several species, which injures books by feeding on the paper and binding. Little is known of them and they are rarely seen either dead or alive. In all probability they cannot stand sunlight. They are essentially borers and their small tunnels often extend through the entire thickness of a book from inner cover to inner cover. Any book suspected of harboring these pests should be promptly isolated and given into the hands of an expert exterminator. (2) A person who is a passionate reader of books.

bosses   Raised brass or other metal pieces on the binding of a book, for protection and ornamentation.

bowdlerized   A word applied to a text altered by the expurgation of words or passages considered offensive or indelicate (by the bowdlerist). The word stems from Dr. Thomas Bowdler (1754–1825), whose name has been associated with various expurgated works, the most famous being *The Family Shakespeare*, which first appeared in the city of Bath, England, in 1807 (twenty plays, in four volumes). No editor's name was given in this edition, but Prof. Noel Perrin, in *Dr. Bowdler's Legacy* (New York: Atheneum, 1969), states, convincingly, that the editor was Dr. Bowdler's sister, Henrietta Maria Bowdler (1757–1830), known to her family as Harriet.

When the next edition of *The Family Shakespeare* appeared (thirty-six plays, in ten volumes) in London, in 1818, Dr. Thomas Bowdler's name was on the title page as the sole editor, and it remained there until the work finally went out of print well over one hundred years later.

Bowker, Richard Rogers (1848–1933)   New York book industry leader, industrial executive, political and civic reformer, news writer and critic. Bowker began contributing to *Publishers Weekly* from the time of its founding in 1872, later became its editor and the owner of its publishing firm, which took his name in 1911. He also devoted immense energy to continuing the improvement of bibliographic tools, developing the library movement, battling for authors' rights and international copyright. In 1876, with *PW's* founder, Frederick Leypoldt (*q.v.*), and Melvil Dewey (*q.v.*) he founded *Library Journal* and aided in founding the American Library Association.

Bowker Lectures on Book Publishing   A series of lectures established in 1935 in memory of Richard Rogers Bowker to provide a forum for the discussion of problems common to authors, publishers, librarians, and readers. The lectures were sponsored jointly by the R. R. Bowker Company and the New York Public Library, and were held annually until 1950, then irregularly until 1967, at the New York Public Library. After a lapse of six years, the series was revived in the fall of 1973 under the new title, Bowker Memorial Lectures on Book Publishing, New Series. The School of Library Service, Columbia University, joined with the Bowker Company to cosponsor the first lecture of the new series. The second lecture, held the following year, was sponsored by Bowker, the New York Public Library, and the School of Library Service, Columbia University. The first seventeen lectures are available in book form from the R.R. Bowker Company.

box On a printed page, featured matter surrounded by rules or white space and placed within or between text columns.

Boydell, John (1719–1804) The London publisher who, with his nephew, Josiah, published the famous illustrated folio edition of Shakespeare's works, printed mainly by William Bulmer (*q.v.*).

Bradford, William (1663–1752) First printer in Philadelphia, 1685. Partner with William Rittenhouse, Samuel Carpenter, and others in establishing the first American paper mill in 1690 near Germantown, Pa. Also first printer in New York City, where he settled in 1693. Buried in Trinity Churchyard, New York.

braille A system of characters invented by Louis Braille (1809–1852) used in printing for the blind. These symbols are embossed or raised in relief so that the reading may be done by the sense of touch with the fingertips.

branching Programming technique by which a computer is made to choose alternative sequences of instructions for execution. An unconditional branch instruction causes the machine to change the sequence of operations from its normal order in every case in which the instruction is encountered. A conditional branch will cause a change in sequence only if some other condition has been met.

brass widths The widths of characters of type. The term "brass" comes from hot metal typesetting systems which use brass matrices of individual characters. In computerized typesetting, brass width tables are set up in memory, and the machine refers to them to obtain data for computing whether a line of type is full or not. *See also* set size.

brayer Printer's or printmaker's hand inking roller.

break; break up To dispose of a form of type that is of no further use by separating material to be remelted from engravings, foundry type, furniture, rules, etc.

breakeven point The number of copies of a book that must be sold in order to recover its costs.

broad-band In data transmission, facilities capable of handling frequency ranges greater than those needed for standard high-grade voice communications. Broad-band transmission is used for very large amounts of data. *See also* data transmission; narrow-band.

broadside A sheet of paper printed on one side only, usually intended to be posted, publicly distributed, or sold. Sometimes called a broadsheet.

brochure A printed and stitched book containing only a few leaves; a pamphlet; a treatise or article published in such form. (From the French "brocher," to stitch.)

brownprint   *See* blueprint.

Brunet, Jacques Charles (1780–1867)   Bibliographer, author of the famous classic in bibliographical literature: *Manuel du Libraire et de L'Amateur de Livres,* 6 volumes, Paris, 1860–65 (5th edition); and *Supplement . . .* by Pierre Deschamps and G. Brunet, 2 volumes, 1878–80. The work, generally referred to as "Brunet," is, despite its age, still an indispensable bibliographical reference book.

brush coated   *See* coated paper.

buckles   In binding: severe wrinkles near the head and back of the folded signatures where the paper is folded at right angles. Also called *gussets.*

buckram   *See* book cloth.

Buenos Aires Convention   *See* all rights reserved.

buffer   An auxiliary computer device that stands between other elements in a system, isolating them and permitting them to operate at their own speeds or in their own sequences without affecting other system elements. Used to match units with dissimilar operating characteristics.

bug   A defect that interferes with proper operation of a system. *See also* debugging.

bulk   (1) The thickness of a book without its cover. (2) To "bulk" a book is to give it the appearance of greater size through the use of thick but light paper. Book papers can "bulk" anywhere from 200 to 2,000 pages to the inch.

Bulmer, William (1758–1830)   Distinguished English printer and bookmaker who printed, under the name of the Shakespeare Press, in partnership with George Nicol and John Boydell the great folio Boydell Shakespeare, issued in nine volumes, 1791–1805.

burin   Engraver's cutting tool.

burnished edges   Colored or gilt edges which have been made smooth and bright by a polishing tool or agate.

Bury, Richard de (1287–1345)   English bibliophile, Bishop of Durham, who collected classical manuscripts and founded a library at Oxford. His famous "Philobiblon" was first printed in 1473, in Cologne.

butted   Lines of type or rules set end to end to make a longer line.

buying around   The practice of buying from a foreign supplier or publisher an edition cheaper than the domestic edition, even though the latter, under publishers' contracts, is supposed to be the only edition offered for sale in the domestic market. Thus, an American library or individual may order from an English book wholesaler books at British (presumably lower) prices, rather than from the authorized U.S. publisher or his suppliers. Publishers on both sides have found the practice difficult to prevent.

byte Sequence of binary bits or digits, shorter than a computer word, normally handled as a unit in the machine. *See also* bit, word.

© Abbreviation symbol for copyright notice required for protection under the Universal Copyright Convention.

c. (1) Abbreviation for the word "copyright" used in descriptive notes, though not legally valid in a copyright notice. (2) Often used as abbreviation for "circa," though for this "ca." is preferred. (3) Invoice symbol for "cancelled."

c & lc Proofreaders' marks calling for the use of capitals and lowercase letters. *See also* Proofreaders' Marks at end of book.

c & sc Proofreaders' marks calling for the use of capitals and small capitals. *See also* Proofreaders' Marks at end of book.

C.B.A. (1) Christian Booksellers Association. (2) Canadian Booksellers Association.

CBI Abbreviation for *Cumulative Book Index*, an international bibliography of books in the English language; published by the H.W. Wilson Company.

ca. Abbreviation for *circa* (*q.v.*).

CIP *See* Cataloging in Publication.

COM Abbreviation for computer-output microfilm.

c.o.r. Abbreviation for "cash on receipt."

CPU Abbreviation for central processing unit.

CRT Abbreviation for cathode-ray tube.

c.w.o. Cash with order. Sometimes used in quoting prices to unknown inquirers.

Caldecott, Randolph (1846–1886) Noted English illustrator of children's books. In the United States the Caldecott Medal for the best picture book of the year was named for him.

calendar An awareness of the differing calendar systems (those of the past, and those now used) is often important in interpreting dates of books, manuscripts, letters, documents, historical events, etc.

Disorders had arisen in the workings of the old Roman calendar, which differed from the Egyptian and Greek forms, and Julius Caesar ordered a restructuring of the Roman calendar then in use to regulate the civil year entirely by the sun. The calendar that Caesar's decree replaced had been a lunar calendar, with an intercalary month. The first Julian Calendar commenced with the first of January in 46 B.C. Because of an error in intercalations, the Julian year was about eleven minutes longer than the astronomical year, and by A.D. 1582 the date of the vernal equinox became displaced by ten days, a figure which increased in the centuries following. The reformation of the Julian Calendar was commissioned by Pope Gregory XIII, and his decree of March 1582 abolished the use of the Julian, and substituted the calendar which has been received in almost all Christian countries, and which came to be known as the *Gregorian Calendar*, or *New Style*. Rome, Spain, Portugal, France, and parts of Italy adopted the new calendar in 1582; the Catholic states in Germany in 1583; the Protestant states, Denmark and Sweden, did not adopt it until 1700; England and her American colonies not until 1752. Russia used the Julian (Old Style) Calendar until 14 February 1918; the Gregorian (New Style) was then adopted, and thirteen days were dropped to make up the time difference.

England reconciled the eleven-day difference in the two calendars at the time of its change from the Old Style to the New Style by a decree ordering the day following 2 September 1752 to be 14 September 1752. At the same time the commencement of the legal year in England was changed from the twenty-fifth of March to the first of January. (The twenty-fifth of March — the Feast of the Annunciation — in medieval times and later, was the beginning of the new year in England through 1752; in Scotland, January 1 had been adopted for New Year's Day beginning with the year 1600.)

The French Revolutionary Calendar of the First French Republic was substituted for the ordinary calendar, dating from the Christian Era, by a decree of the National Convention in 1793. The date of the beginning of the new calendar was set for 22 September 1792, the day from which the existence of the Republic was reckoned. The year, beginning at midnight of the day of the autumnal equinox, was divided into twelve months of thirty days, with five additional days for festivals, and six in every fourth year. Each month was divided into three decades of ten days each, the week being abolished. The calendar years were numbered *An I* (22 September 1792 to 21 September 1793) through *An XIV* (23 September 1805 to 22 December 1805). The calendar was abolished by Napoleon in favor of the ordinary one at the end of the year 1805.

The Hebrew (Jewish) Calendar is a lunisolar calendar, reckoning from the year 3761 B.C., the date traditionally given for the Creation.

The Mohammedan Calendar, a lunar calendar, reckons from the year of the hegira (the flight of Mohammed from Mecca), which took place in A.D. 622.

calendering Process of polishing newly made paper between smooth cylinders under pressure and sometimes heat to make its surface smooth. Paper which receives a minimum of calendering emerges as an antique.

With more calendering it acquires a machine finish, then an English finish, and it finally becomes a super-calendered sheet which has a glossy finish.

calf   Calfskin prepared and used for bindings on books.

California job case   *See* case.

called for   Antiquarian term used to describe a book with reference to a criterion laid down by some authority, named or unnamed. For example, a book may be described as being "without the frontispiece called for by Blanck"; or, "with the leaf before the title called for by Storm."

calligraphy   Literally, from the Greek, "beautiful handwriting"; writing as an art. In calligraphy, the letter forms are both inspired and limited by the writing tool—ordinarily the broad-point pen, but occasionally the Spencerian pen, the brush (as in oriental writing), and even the crayon.

calotype   Early photographic process (ca. 1839) invented by William Henry Fox Talbot, also called Talbotype. Paper sensitized with silver iodide was brushed over with solution of silver nitrate, acetic and gallic acids and exposed while wet. Translucent paper permitted a positive to be printed and led to the use of the glass plate.

cameo binding   A binding with a cameo-like decoration, usually inset or stamped on front cover.

camera   In printing, a special large camera used to photograph art, illustrations, photographs, paste-ups, or other copy in preparation for stripping the film negatives or positives into flats. Such graphic arts cameras are used to make both halftone and line shots. *See also* strip in; flat; halftone; line drawing.

camera-ready   Said of artwork, illustrations, paste-ups of type pages, or other materials that are completely ready to be photographed on a graphic arts camera, preparatory to stripping into flats. *See also* camera; strip in; flat.

Cameron Book Production System   Brand name for a commercial model of the belt press (*q.v.*).

cancel; cancellans   A new leaf or signature reprinted and inserted because of errors or defects in the leaf or signature replaced. In general, any printed matter substituted for that stricken out.

cancelland; cancellandum   The excised portion of a book; usually a single leaf bearing an error.

caps and small caps (c & sc)   CAPITALS and SMALL CAPITALS in fonts of type. Directions for the compositor to set in small capitals, with the initial letters in large capitals. *See also* Proofreaders' Marks at end of book.

caption (1) The brief title or description which identifies or explains an illustration. (2) Less frequently: a headline, as of a chapter, table, etc. *See also* legend.

card reader A device for sensing data encoded on a punch card and entering it in the computer. *See also* punch card; read.

carding out Extending a column of type by means of strips of card stock or paper, when the thinnest metal spacing material would be too thick.

caret The sign ∧ used to indicate an insertion is to be made. *See also* Proofreaders' Marks at end of book.

Carey, Mathew (1760–1839) Leading publisher and bookseller in the United States in its formative period. He migrated to Philadelphia from Ireland in 1784, published magazines, organized aggressive methods of selling books including subscription and itinerant bookselling (one of his salesmen was Parson Weems (*q.v.*). Carey made the first experiments in an American commercial book fair and helped found the first U.S. booksellers' association, 1806. His and his son's firm, Carey & Lea, survives as Lea & Febiger.

carriage Cost of transportation of merchandise from publisher to dealer.

cartouche Scroll-like flourish with a pen or brush, used as an ornamental border or frame.

cartridge A container for magnetic tape, similar to a *cassette* (*q.v.*).

case (1) A preassembled hard cover for a book which comprises the front and back covers and connecting material across the spine, and wraps around the inside pages. *Casing-in* is the binder's term for inserting the book, when sewed, into its case. Cf. slipcase. (2) Compartmented tray in which hand type is kept. The capital letters used to be kept in the upper case, small letters in the lower. The so-called *California job case* accommodates both side by side. *See also* lowercase; uppercase.

case binding (1) A hard cover that has been put around a book in a preassembled piece. (In fine hand binding the cover is usually assembled right on the book, instead of separately.) (2) The process of binding hardcover books.

Caslon, William (1692–1766) Famous English type designer and type founder. Designed and cast the types which bear his name, the most widely used of type designs in English and American printing. Originally famed as an engraver of gunbarrels, he began type founding in 1720, and in 1734 he issued his famous specimen book of typefaces.

cassette (1) In tape recording, a standard container with two spools that holds magnetic recording tape. First designed for audio recording with tape recorders, such cassettes are now being used in digital data handling systems as a means of storage. (2) In phototypesetting, a portable container for light-sensitive material. The cassette usually attaches directly to the typesetting machine either to feed or receive material.

cast coated *See* coated paper.

cast off To estimate the number of pages or columns of type a given amount of copy will make.

casting The process of flowing molten metal against a matrix in a mold and allowing it to cool and harden for the purpose of producing individual types, lines of type, or *stereotypes*.

Cataloging in Publication (CIP) A program established by the Library of Congress in July 1971, wherein participating publishers provide the Library of Congress with galleys and/or descriptive front matter from their books from which professional cataloging data is prepared by L.C. and returned to the publisher. This CIP Data is usually printed on the verso of the title page. Because CIP reduces cataloging costs and speeds the delivery of books to readers, the program is benefiting the library world and the publishing industry alike. In general, the program's scope includes all U.S. trade monographs from members of the Association of American Publishers, the Association of American University Presses, and other trade book publishers. As of 1974, publications of selected government agencies are also included in the program.

catchline On proofs, a temporary, identifying headline.

catchword (1) In old books the word placed at the bottom of each page, under the last word in the last line, being the first word of the following page. It was designed to assist the printer in imposition and the binder in gathering the signatures. (2) A word at the head of a page or column to indicate the contents, as in a dictionary.

catchword entry The entry of a title in an index, list, or catalog by its most important or most easily remembered word. Also known as an *inverted entry*.

cathode-ray tube An electronic vacuum tube similar to that used in television sets as picture tubes. Images are displayed on the face or "screen." In typesetting machines, type characters are displayed at extremely high speeds and the light thus generated is used to expose photographic materials. In editing and layout terminals, type is displayed for reading by the operator. *See also* character generation; video editing terminal; video layout terminal.

Caxton, William (1422?–1491)   The first English printer. He was apprenticed in 1438 to a London silk merchant; merchant on his own account at Bruges (1446–1470); Governor of English merchants in the Low Countries (1465–1469), with rank and duties similar to those of a British consul or ambassador. After resigning his office as Governor in March 1469 he began a translation of Raoul Le Fèvre's *Recueil des Histoires de Troi*, which he finished at the request of Duchess Margaret of Burgundy in 1471. He found it impossible to prepare sufficient manuscript copies to meet the demand, and during a five-month visit to Cologne in 1471–1472, he learned something of the new art of printing. He then established a printing press of his own at Bruges, in partnership with Colard Mansion. His first book was his own translation of the *Recueil*, named in English *The Recuyell of the Historyes of Troye*. The work is undated, and bears no place of printing, but most authorities agree that it was printed at Bruges sometime between 1472 and 1474. He printed another translation at Bruges, *The Game and Playe of the Chesse*. He returned to England in the autumn of 1476 and established a press at Westminster, using type and equipment brought over from Bruges. The first known *dated* book printed by Caxton was issued by him at Westminster on the 18th of November 1477; the work was a translation from the French by Caxton's friend Lord Rivers, titled *Dictes and Sayengis of the Philosophers.*

Between 1476 and his death in 1491 Caxton printed about one hundred books. The most notable of these were his folio editions of Chaucer's *Canterbury Tales* (1478), *Chronicles of England* (1480), Higden's *Polychronicon* (1481), Gower's *Confessio Amantis* (1483), Voragine's *Golden Legend* (1484), and Malory's *Morte D'Arthur* (1485). *See also* Worde, Wynkyn de.

censor; censorship   A censor may be a person, persons, or body empowered by law to prohibit the production, distribution, or sale of materials believed to be objectionable for reasons of politics, obscenity, or blasphemy; a censor may also be a self-appointed person or group bringing pressure upon retailers, distributors, exhibitors, educators, librarians, publishers, the press, and public, to excise or suppress material the censor finds offensive. Censorship is the act of the censor; e.g., the removal of an offending publication from display, circulation, or sale, barring it from schools, from the mail or from passage through customs, ordinarily by means of administrative or court order. The term "prior censorship" is applied to the excision or suppression of material prior to publication or distribution. Censorship is distinguished from selection, as in the choosing of books for bookstore or library stocks, a process in which the censor's criteria do not or should not apply.

centered dot   A period placed higher than the base line of the typeface. Used to separate syllables (syl·lab·i·ca·tion), to show multiplication (2·

$2 = 4$), to separate roman capitals in the classic form of tablet inscriptions (M·A·R·C·V·S A·N·T·O·N·I·V·S). Sometimes called a *space dot.*

central processing unit   The central section of a computer which actually performs the active data processing procedures. The CPU generally contains the main or core memory, all arithmetic units, and special registers for handling data.

Cerf, Bennett Alfred (1898–1971)   Publisher-publicist, co-founder of Random House (with Donald S. Klopfer). Cerf and Klopfer purchased Modern Library in 1925, and founded Random House in 1927; Cerf was president to 1965, then chairman to 1970. The firm emphasized fine design, developed major U.S. and foreign writers, aggressively merchandized Modern Library, and launched innovative lines for children and young people. The firm's defense of Joyce's *Ulysses* resulted in a landmark anticensorship decision in 1933. Uniquely among publishers, Cerf lectured constantly on books and humor, toured bookstores and colleges, wrote gossipy, book-centered columns, and was a star of radio and TV shows.

chain-lines   In *laid paper* (*q.v.*), the widely spaced lines which become visible when the paper is held up to the light. Also known as chain-marks.

chain printer   A computer-operated device that types out material in a computer onto a continuous length of paper. Individual type characters are mounted on an endless chain which rotates past the points of impact. As the proper character passes the position desired, it is struck onto the paper. Such machines operate at very high speeds compared to conventional typewriters.

chained books   Books chained to the shelves of university, monastic, and other libraries to prevent theft in the early days of printing.

channel   A path for the transmission of data electronically. In punched paper or magnetic tapes, each row of holes or electrical impulses is considered a channel, and tapes are referred to by the number of channels they hold—six channel, seven channel, etc. *See also* level.

chapbook   From the Anglo-Saxon root "ceap," trade. Small, cheap book, in a paper binding, popular in England and the American Colonies in the seventeenth and eighteenth centuries, containing tales, ballads, lives, tracts, and topical material. Sold by chapmen, i.e., peddlers, hawkers.

chapel   The workmen in a printing office, considered as a society. As used in the United States, the term applies to an organization of the union printers employed in a printing house.

chapter heading   Heading printed at the beginning of each chapter above the text.

character (1) A letter of the alphabet, a numeral, mark of punctuation, or any other symbol used in typesetting. In making a "character count," spaces count as one. (2) A defined unit of information stored in and handled by a computer.

character generation Projection or construction of typographic images on the face of a cathode-ray tube. Such systems permit electronic manipulation of characters, such as the making of an italic out of a roman letter. Also, some systems store characters in digital form by breaking them up into thousands of discrete electronic pulses. This further enables the designs to be changed via computer programming techniques. Character generation typesetting machines can operate at extremely high speeds.

character recognition Use of a machine to sense and encode into machine language characters that are handwritten, typed, printed, or otherwise indicated graphically. *See also* optical character recognition.

character set (1) A specific group of characters acceptable to a computer system, which it has been programmed to handle. (2) In typography, the lateral width of individual characters. *See also* set size.

character style Distinguishing design or characteristics of a typeface.

chase Steel frame in which type in pages is locked up for placing on the press, or for the foundry when plates are to be made.

checklist A list of books, pamphlets, or other material with a minimum of bibliographical description of the works recorded.

chemical pulp The raw material from which the better grades of book papers are made. Chemical pulp is made from wood fibers chemically treated to remove the harmful ingredients that cause newsprint (made from groundwood pulp) to become yellow and brittle with age. Paper made from chemical pulp without any admixture of groundwood pulp is called a "free sheet," i.e., free of groundwood.

Children's Book Week *See* Book Week.

China paper A thin, soft paper, of a faint yellowish or brownish tint, prepared from the bark of the bamboo. It is much used for fine impressions from wood engravings, and occasionally for proofs from steel-plate engravings, etc.

Chinese (or Japanese) style Said of a book in which each leaf is double thick and uncut, with the interior blank. Books copied on the Xerox Copyflo come out on one side of an endless web, which is then accordion folded and bound in this style.

chip board A less expensive substitute for *binder's board* (*q.v.*).

Chiswick Press Founded in 1811 by Charles Whittingham (1767–1840), at Chiswick, a largely residential district suburban to London. Whittingham was a printer of considerable merit who was famous for a number of small books with brilliantly printed woodcuts, and as the printer of attractive popular-priced classics. He was the first to print India paper editions. His nephew, Charles Whittingham, the Younger (1795–1876), worked with his uncle from 1824 to 1828, and he took over the Chiswick Press upon the death of his uncle in 1840. He himself was an excellent printer, and he formed an association with William Pickering for whom he did much printing after 1830. After the younger Whittingham's death in 1876, the Chiswick Press was taken over by George Bell. It was at this press that William Morris made his experiments in printing, before setting up his own Kelmscott Press in 1891.

chrestomathy A collection of choice passages from an author or authors.

circa (ca.) Latin word for *about, around*; often used in English with numerals to denote approximate accuracy, e.g., "printed circa 1747."

circuit A system of electrical components and conductors through which electrical current can flow. In communications, a link between two points.

circuit edges *See* divinity circuit.

circulating library *See* rental library.

cities, classical names of Names used in the colophons or on the title pages of old books may be found, with their modern equivalents, in the "Dictionnaire de Geographique Ancienne et Moderne," by P. Deschamps, facsimile edition, 1922, Paris & Berlin; also in "Place Names in Imprints," by R. A. Peddie, 1932, Grafton, London; and in the "Columbia Lippincott Gazetteer of the World," edited by Leon E. Seltzer, 1952, Columbia University Press.

class "A" library binding One which meets certain standards set by the Library Binding Institute and the American Library Association.

classified catalog A catalog arranged by a numeric or alphabetic notation according to subject content. Also called classed catalog, or class catalog. Cf. dictionary catalog.

clean tape A tape containing only the codes required to operate a typesetting machine, with all errors and extraneous codes removed.

clear To return a computer memory and computation circuits to their original state prior to the start of processing operations.

cleat sewing   *See* sewing.

clipping bureau   An organization which makes a business of collecting personal notices, book reviews, etc., from current newspapers and periodicals and furnishing them for a fee to the persons concerned.

close up   To push type closer together by replacing thicker with thinner spaces.

closed-loop system   System in which all operations, once started, take place automatically until the end result is reached, without human intervention. *See* loop; open-loop system.

cloth   The commonest material used for the binding, or casing, of books. A book described as "cloth" means, unless otherwise indicated, cloth pasted over stiff boards. *See also* book cloth.

coated paper   Paper surfaced with white clay or a similar substance to provide a smooth printing surface. Coated papers called *enamel* are glossy, but there are also grades of *dull-coated*. The cheaper coated papers have the coating applied right in the papermaking machine and are called *machine coated*. When the coating is applied as a separate and later operation, the process is called *brush coating*. Papers having extra high gloss are called *cast coated*.

Cobden-Sanderson, T. J. (1840–1922)   Founder of the Doves Press (*q.v.*) at Hammersmith, England; also ranks as one of the great bookbinders of modern times.

Cochin, Charles Nicolas (1715–1790)   The most celebrated of a prominent family of French engravers and painters. He was one of the first to produce engraved title pages, which were imitated up to the end of the eighteenth century by all who followed. He provided engravings for editions of La Fontaine, Rousseau, Boccaccio, Tasso, and Ariosto.

cockle   The puckered effect on paper, naturally or artificially produced in the drying process.

code   A system of symbols for representing various other types of data or instructions in a computerized system.

code set   The coded representation of a given character set.

codex (*pl.* **codices;** *abbr.* **cod.;** *pl.* **codd.**)   Manuscript in book form. It owed its existence to the substitution of vellum for papyrus as the common writing material for Greek and Roman literature; vellum was a tough material capable of being inscribed on both sides, and the leaves could be stitched and bound in a form similar to books of modern times. The earliest great vellum Greek codices of the Bible, and of Latin classical authors, dating back to the fourth century, are composed of very finely prepared material; some fragments of the codox form of manuscript exist which show that the form was already in use in the first centuries of our era. More than one hundred Bible manuscripts in codex form, dating from the fourth century to the tenth century, written in uncial characters, are known; more than 1,200 dating from the ninth to the sixteenth centuries, written in cursive characters, are known.

Among the famous Bible codices are the *Alexandrian Codex*, a fifth century manuscript in Greek of the Scriptures (containing the New Testament, nearly complete), which had belonged to the library of the patriarchs of Alexandria, in Africa, A.D. 1098, and which, in 1627 was sent as a present to King Charles I. Since 1757 it has been in the British Museum; and the *Codex Sinaiticus*, a fourteenth century manuscript in Greek (containing the New Testament, twenty-six Books of the Old Testament, and the Apocrypha), which was the great discovery of Lobegott Friedrich K. von Tischendorf, the German biblical scholar and critic (1815–1874), at the monastery at Mount Sinai, in 1844, and a larger portion in 1859. The first portion was given to the Leipzig Library, where it still is; the second, and larger portion, was presented to the Russian Czar at St. Petersburg (who was patron of the monastery). This larger portion was acquired by the British Museum in 1933 for £100,000.

cold type Composition produced on a direct-impression typewriter-like machine; struck-image composition. Preferred usage of this term eliminates both hot metal and photographic composition processes, although photo-composition is sometimes erroneously called cold type. *See also* photocomposition; direct-impression; struck-image.

Colines, Simon de (1475–1547) Printer and scholar, who served as foreman in the printing house of Henri Estienne (*q.v*) and who continued the firm after Estienne's death in 1521. Colines married Estienne's widow and assumed management of the printing plant. His correct texts and fine typography brought fame to the establishment; he printed more than 500 various editions, many of them illustrated, and the house of Estienne was most influential in the French printing renaissance and in the movement to replace gothic types with roman. Colines had recognized the genius of Geoffroy Tory and employed him to design decorations and types for use at the press; he became known for the excellence of his Greek types, and he was the first to use italic types in France.

collate (1) To examine the gathered signatures of a book in order to verify their full count and arrangement. Rare books are collated to verify completeness, including plates, leaves, etc. (2) In binding, to assemble individual sheets or leaves into complete sets, as opposed to gathering which is the assembly of signatures into complete sets. Collating is done primarily in the binding of smaller booklets, pamphlets, and loose-leaf products. *See also* gathering.

collating mark   A short rule or dot inserted in the form to appear on the back fold of each signature of a book, for use in checking the accuracy of gathering. The mark on the first signature appears near the top, that on the second a little lower, the third still lower, etc. When the signatures are gathered for binding the marks appear in a diagonal arrangement which would be broken if a signature were duplicated, out of place, or omitted. The older system of marking each signature on the first page with a number, letter or other symbol is still used in England and to some extent in the United States.

collected edition   The book publication of the works of an author in uniform style. If the books were originally published by several firms, one publisher makes an arrangement with all to publish a uniform edition. A collected edition is not necessarily a complete edition.

collotype   *See* photogelatin.

colophon   From the Greek "kolophon," finishing touch. (1) The inscription which the letterer or printer placed at the end of a manuscript or book, with the facts about its production, author, date, title, etc. In late bookmaking the title page has largely taken the place of the colophon for recording these details with regard to publication. In many modern books of special typography the use of a colophon has been revived as a place of record for the typographical details. (2) Also frequently but incorrectly used to mean the trade emblem or device of a printer or publisher.

color printing   In printers' parlance, black is a "color" and a "one-color job" is usually a black-and-white job. A job printed in black and red thus becomes a two-color job, and a job printed in red, yellow, blue, and black becomes a four-color job. There is an important difference, however, between *multicolor printing* and *full-color printing*. In multicolor printing, the printer carefully mixes inks to match each distinguishable color in the art work. In full color the inks he uses may have no apparent relation to the art work (they are usually yellow, cyan, magenta, and black) but they have been carefully chosen so that when scientifically combined by *process color* (*q.v.*) techniques they can reproduce the full range of browns, grays, greens, purples, etc.

color separation   *See* process color.

colporteur A traveling book agent, usually of a religious group or society, who sells low-priced tracts.

column inch A measure of space on a type page, one inch deep and as wide as a column.

combination plate Plate in which both line and halftone techniques are combined.

command An instruction or control signal in machine language.

communications format *See* bibliographic information interchange format.

compatibility The ability of one computerized system to accept and handle data from another system. The ability of one set of equipment and programs to be included in a system with other equipment and programs.

compose To set type to be printed. *Compositor*, a person who sets type; *composition*, the process of setting type or the type set; *composing room*, room where type is set; *composing stick*, a metal tool in which type is set.

computer A device that accepts data, applies programmed sets of processing procedures to it, and produces the results in some usable form. All computers consist, in one form or another, of input and output facilities, storage, arithmetic, and logical processing, memory, and a control section.

computer graphics Computer-generated images other than single character symbols. Included are charts, diagrams, drawings, and other pictorial representations.

computer-output microfilm Microfilm exposed in a special high-speed character generator called a COM unit.

computer word *See* word.

Comstock, Anthony (1844–1915) Founder in 1873 of the New York Society for the Suppression of Vice, and instrumental in securing to the U.S. Post Office the power to judge and exclude obscene books from the mails.

concordance An alphabetical index of words showing the places in the text of a book or an author's complete works where each may be found.

concurrent processing Ability of a computer to work on more than one program or task at the same time.

condensed A narrower and more compact version of a type design.

configuration A group of machines interconnected and programmed to work as a single integrated system.

conjugate   A leaf comprising either half of a four-page sheet. For example: in a 16-page signature pages 1-2 (leaf 1) would be the conjugate of pages 15-16 (leaf 8) and vice versa.

consignment   *See* on consignment.

console   A control station in a computer system providing various manual controls which may be used to manually alter the system's operation.

contacting   In photography, the process of exposing one piece of photographic material from an image on another piece by placing them physically in tight contact with each other and shining light through the image. Contacting provides duplicate images in a size ratio of one to one only.

contemporary binding   Binding executed in the period of publication of the book.

continuation   A publication issued as part of a series, or as a supplement to an earlier work.

continuation order   *See* standing order.

continuous tape   Synonym for raw tape, idiot tape (*q.v.*).

continuous tone   Photographic image in which density of the gray and black areas varies continuously between various shades or tone values, as opposed to a "line" image in which density varies intermittently. The halftone process used to reproduce continuous tone images in printing actually converts the continuous tone areas to line images which create an optical illusion of continuous tones. *See also* halftone.

control unit   Section of a computer which directs all other operations in the system on instructions from the program.

conversion   (1) Changing data from one form to another, such as converting data from one machine language to another, or converting material from magnetic tape storage into phototypeset pages. (2) Changing of a system from one type of equipment or programming to another.

cooperative advertising   Arrangement whereby publisher and bookseller split advertising costs, the publisher's books being promoted over the dealer's name. *See also* allowance.

cooperative publishing   *See* vanity publishers.

coordinate digitizing   Method of defining location of elements in a two-dimensional area by use of *x–y* coordinates. Any position on a grid can be defined by two numbers, one for the vertical *x* scale and one for the horizontal *y* scale. Using such data on position, a computer can make up complete typographic arrangements and produce all required instructions for a phototypesetting unit to expose all type in proper position on a page. *See also* grid; grid coordinate system.

copperplate engraving The process of intaglio engraving on copper for reproduction, or the print resulting from it. *See also* engraving.

copy (1) A specimen of a given book. (2) Printer's term for manuscript presented for setting in type. (3) Also used to designate all art or illustration material sent to the printer, such as photographs and drawings. (4) A computer operation in which data is taken from memory and transported elsewhere, but the original record of the data is retained in memory and not erased. *See also* erase.

copy block Unit of composition which is naturally handled as a cohesive single element, although it may contain a number of type lines and styles. *See also* area composition.

copy edit To check a manuscript, before marking copy for printer, for *house style* (*q.v.*), accuracy of fact, spelling, syntax, logical construction, possible libel, etc.

copy fitting Adjusting copy to space allotted, before sending to printer. This may be done by changing the space allotment, the length of copy, or the size or arrangement of type.

copy preparation The act of preparing for the compositor a manuscript which has been copy edited (*q.v.*). It includes making the manuscript legible and accurate, indicating style, type, etc.

copyholder One who reads copy to a proofreader.

copyright Copyright is literary, dramatic, artistic, and musical property protection as authorized by the United States Constitution, "securing for limited Times to Authors . . . the exclusive Right to their respective Writings . . . ." (Article I, Sect. 8) Copyright of books under the code of 1909 depends upon publication with notice of copyright printed on the title page or verso, and consisting of the following elements: (a) The word *copyright*, the abbreviation *Copr.*, or the symbol ©. Use of the symbol © may result in securing copyright in some countries outside of the United States under the provisions of the Universal Copyright Convention (*q.v.*); (b) The name of the copyright owner; (c) The date of publication. The elements of the notice should all appear together, for example: © John Doe 1974.

To comply with the law concerning copyright for books, the following steps must be taken: (a) produce copies containing the copyright notice; (b) publish the book; (c) register the copyright claim with the Register of Copyrights by depositing two copies of the work as published with the copyright notice, accompanied by a six-dollar registration fee.

Once a work has been published without the required copyright notice, copyright protection is lost permanently and cannot be regained. Adding the correct notice later will not restore protection nor permit the Copyright Office to register a claim.

The original term of copyright lasts for twenty-eight years, and may be renewed for twenty-eight years if applied for by the author or his heirs. During recent Congressional efforts to revise the U.S. copyright law, Congress has extended the second term of copyright eight times, so that all second-term copyrights scheduled to expire between September 19, 1962, and December 31, 1973, have been extended to the end of 1974.

For further information, the pamphlet, *Copyright Law of the United States of America*, revised, 1973, is available from the Superintendent of Documents, U.S. Government Printing Office.

copyright, ad interim A short-term copyright, lasting for a maximum of five years, for the protection of books and periodicals in the English language manufactured and first published outside of the United States. Ad interim copyright may be secured by depositing with the Copyright Office one complete copy of the foreign edition within six months of its publication abroad, with a request for the reservation of the copyright and a statement of the name and nationality of the author and of the copyright proprietor, and the date of publication. The law permits the importation of 1,500 copies of works for which ad interim registration has been made. The copyright may be extended to the full copyright term of twenty-eight years if an American edition of the work is manufactured and published with copyright notice during the five-year period of ad interim copyright, and if a claim covering the American edition is registered.

copyright, British Under the United Kingdom Copyright Act of 1956, copyright subsists automatically in every original literary, dramatic, musical, or artistic work if, (a) in the case of an *unpublished* work, the author was a "qualified" person (e.g., a British subject, or a subject of a country to which the provisions of the Act have been applied) at the time the work was made, or (b) in the case of a *published* work, the first publication took place in the United Kingdom or in another country to which the Act has been extended or applied, or the author was a "qualified" person at the time the work was first published. The term of copyright extends for life and fifty years.

copyright, Canadian Under the amended act of 1931, copyright in Canada is on the same general lines as British copyright, but for authors of the United States and other non-Union countries there is involved the possibility of republication in Canada under government license if the copyright owner does not himself manufacture his edition in Canada. This provision is in retaliation for the United States manufacturing requirements but has not been used.

copyright, common law The unpublished works of authors, alien or domestic, if not voluntarily registered in the Copyright Office, are protected under the common law. This protection is unlimited and free from formalities.

copyright, inter-American Copyright relations among the countries of the Western Hemisphere make up a confused network of agreements, beginning with the Montevideo Convention of 1886. Most widely effective is the Buenos Aires Convention of 1910, signed by seventeen countries. Several countries in the Western Hemisphere, including Argentina, Brazil, Canada, Mexico, and Uruguay, are members of the Berne Convention (*q.v.*). Many are also members of the Universal Copyright Convention (*q.v.*), including Argentina, Brazil, Canada, Chile, Costa Rica, Cuba, Ecuador, Guatemala, Haiti, Mexico, Nicaragua, Panama, Paraguay, Peru, United States, Venezuela.

copyright, international *See* Berne Convention; Universal Copyright Convention.

copyright fees The fee for registration of any published work subject to copyright is two copies of the book and six dollars. (The same for a set of volumes deposited at the same time.) This includes the Copyright Office certificate under seal.

Copyright claims in works by foreign authors may be registered without payment of the six-dollar registration fee in the following circumstances: the work has been published (copies placed on sale, sold, or publicly distributed); and first publication occurred outside the United States; and the author was not a United States citizen or resident on the date of first publication; and two copies of the published work are sent to the Copyright Office within six months of the date of first publication, together with a completed application and a completed catalog card.

core storage Tiny doughnut-shaped iron rings that can be magnetized or demagnetized to record presence or absence of data. *See also* magnetic storage; random access storage.

corporate entry Catalog or index entry under the name of an organization or institution, rather than an individual.

corrigenda *See* errata.

Coster of Haarlem *See* movable type.

cottage style   A seventeenth century style of ornamentation developed by Samuel Mearne, binder to King Charles II. In popular use on Bibles and prayer books. So called because the four corners and lines of parallel-line rectangles used to decorate panels break outward, resembling the gables of cottages.

covers bound in   The original covers included within a later binding. Occasionally the covers are preserved when the volume is rebound by mounting them as flyleaves or using them as endpapers.

cradle books   *See* incunabula.

crash   Synonym for *super*, applied in the backing process. *See also* lining.

creasing   Compressing the fibers of paper along a line where a fold is to be made. Done on either a regular printing press, a special cutting and creasing press, or a folding machine by impressing a raised rule or disk against the paper. The creasing not only locates and facilitates the fold, but also increases the number of times the paper can be flexed at the crease before breaking. *See also* scoring.

credit line   A statement giving the name of a photographer, artist, author, agency, or publication responsible for the picture, photograph, article, or quotation which is being used.

crop   To trim off. A photograph is "cropped" when part of the top, bottom, or sides is omitted from its reproduction, in order to improve its composition or bring it into proper proportions for the space it is to occupy. A book is said to be "cropped" when the margins have been cut so close that the printing or illustrations have been damaged.

cross-reference   A reference made from one part of a book to another, or from one catalog entry to another.

cross-reference, general   Notation under one catalog heading as to where the user may expect to find certain types of entries. For example, a note under the heading "dogs" might read "Here are entered general works on dogs; for information on a particular breed, see name of breed."

crown octavo; crown quarto   *See* book sizes.

crushed levant   Levant morocco, the surface of which has been crushed down and polished.

cum licentia   Latin for "with permission." A notice in a book signifying that it is published by leave of the authorities, either secular or ecclesiastical. *See also* cum privilegio; nihil obstat; imprimatur.

cum privilegio   Latin for "with permission." Not in practical use now, but may be found in old books, signifying approval of authority, either secular or ecclesiastical. *See also* cum licentia; nihil obstat; imprimatur.

cumulative index   An index in periodical form, which combines successively the entries of earlier issues or volumes into a single index.

cuneiform writing   Wedge-shaped characters, impressed in clay and baked, used by the ancient Assyrians and Babylonians. Thought to have originated 6,000 years ago, remaining in use until the third century B.C.

curiosa   Term used in classifying books of curious and unusual subject matter. Sometimes used euphemistically as a classification for *erotica* (*q.v.*) *See also* facetiae; pornography.

cursive   (1) Running, flowing, from the Latin meaning coursing. Specifically applied to early writing and lettering on manuscripts. The cursive letters have the strokes joined and letters rounded. (2) American term for certain faces similar to, but more decorative than, italic.

cursor   A spot of light on the face of a video display screen telling the operator where the computer will perform its next operations. The operator can move the cursor to any desired spot on the screen by tapping control keys. An alternative to the cursor is the use of a light pen. *See also* light pen.

custom book   A book assembled from a large variety of available materials specifically to the customer's order. Used to some extent now in higher education by a teacher who may choose a set of text materials and then have it manufactured as a textbook in very small quantities for his classes. Under one scheme, the teacher may choose any existing materials so long as permissions to reprint can be obtained by the publisher. In another scheme, the publisher offers a predetermined set of materials from which the teacher may choose.

custom-bound   Bound to order.

cut   (1) Term sometimes used to mean any printed illustration. (2) Also the *engraving* or *plate* from which (in letterpress) it is printed.

cut dummy   Complete proofs of the illustrations of a book, arranged in proper sequence and containing the figure and galley numbers.

cut edges   One or more edges of a book trimmed by machinery.

cut flush   To trim the cover of a book even with its edges.

cut-in   Set into the type page in such a way that there is type matter on three sides.

cycle Time interval required by a computerized system to complete a given set of events and return to a state at which it is ready to start another set of operations.

cylinder press *See* flat-bed cylinder press.

d.s. (*pl.* **ds. s.**) Document signed. A document printed or in the hand of a person other than the signer.

d.w. Dust wrapper. *See* dust jacket.

dandy roll In papermaking: a cylinder of wire gauze which presses upon the drained but still moist pulp just before it starts through the rollers. The weaving of the wire of the dandy roll leaves its impression on the paper and determines whether it is to be wove paper (with the impression of fine even gauze) or laid paper (with the impression of parallel lines).

When designs or monograms are incorporated into the fine wire of the roll, *watermarks* are produced.

data Alphabetic and numeric characters, facts, etc., which are processed by a computer.

data bank A collection of data stored in a computer system in such a way that it can be extracted in many ways to form different compilations for various purposes.

data collection Process of collecting and transmitting data from a number of outlying remote positions to a central point.

data processing Manipulation of data according to prespecified rules to achieve predetermined results.

data reduction Transforming large volumes of raw data, via processing, into more useful condensations or simplifications.

data transmission Sending of coded data over communications links such as telephone lines at high speeds. *See also* broad-band.

dating An extension of the period of credit usually allowed by a supplier (e.g., a publisher) to a retailer.

Daye, Stephen (1594–1668) Originally a locksmith by trade. In 1639 he took charge of the first printing press in the English colonies in America at Cambridge, Massachusetts. The press had been obtained for the colony by Rev. Jose Glover, who died in 1638 on his voyage to America from England with the press. The first publication of the press in January 1639 was a broadside, *The Oath of a Free-Man*, of which no copy is known; the second was *An Almanack, Calculated for New England*, by William Pierce, also in 1639. No copy of this is known. In 1640, Daye produced *The Whole Booke of Psalmes,* commonly known as *The Bay Psalm Book* (*q.v.*), the earliest work printed in the United States known to be extant.

de luxe   A French term meaning, literally, of elegance. Applied to editions finely printed on superior paper—usually limited in number.

dead matter   Set type no longer needed for printing. Cf. live matter.

debugging   The process of discovering and eliminating errors in computer programs or detection and correction of malfunctions in equipment. *See also* bug.

decimal classification   *See* Dewey decimal classification.

deck   A collection of punched cards containing a set of coded data. *See* storage.

deckle edge   The rough edge on a sheet of paper where the pulp flowed under the frame while still liquid. The frame which forms the border of a hand mold is called the deckle, also the rubber strip that confines the flowing pulp on the screen of a paper machine.

These rough edges are often left untrimmed in the making of books from handmade paper. In machine-made paper, deckle is not obtainable on four sides but a deckle effect can be imitated.

decision   In a computer, the process of comparing two sets of data and choosing among alternative operations to perform based on the results of the comparison.

decoding   Interpreting the coded data and instructions in a computer system in order to act upon them. A computer will so interpret instruction codes to trigger subsequent processing routines, for example.

dedication   An inscription to honor or compliment someone, usually a patron, relative, or friend. The dedication is usually on the first leaf following the title page of a book. *See also* front matter.

definitive edition   An edition said to be the most authoritative version of a work.

de Graff, Robert Fair (1895–) Publisher who founded the modern American paperback industry. After successfully developing reprint lines for Doubleday, 1922–36, and the Blue Ribbon Books reprints, he founded Pocket Books, Inc., in 1938, believing that pocket-sized, brightly papercovered, twenty-five-cent reprints of good fiction and occasional nonfiction would have wide appeal. Keys to successful operation were mass production printing on rotary presses, combined with distribution through the magazine wholesale system. Simon & Schuster, early backers of the enterprise, bought controlling interest in Pocket Books in 1967.

delete; dele   To remove; omit. A mark used in correcting proof, like the Greek letter δ, put in the margin to show that certain characters or words marked in the line opposite are to be omitted. *See also* Proofreaders' Marks at end of book.

demy octavo; demy quarto   *See* book sizes.

densitometer   A most widely used quality control instrument in all reproductive processes based on photography and electronic technologies. Applicable to the evaluation of most original subjects, photographic intermediates in black-on-white, paper, printing inks, as well as final printed images of most kinds, including process color jobs.

density   (1) In a computer system, the amount of data that can be stored in a given area of memory. (2) In photography, the degree of opacity in a piece of photosensitive material. (3) In typography, the number of type characters fitted into a given area.

dentelle   French word for lace. Used to describe lace-like patterns which the binder applies by tool or wheel to the outer or inner borders of a binding.

deposit copies   Copies of a newly published book deposited in specified libraries under national copyright law in the United States, Great Britain, Canada, Italy, etc.

Derôme   French family in the eighteenth century which added several illustrious names to the art of binding of that period. The most famous was Nicolas Derôme, known as Derôme le jeune (1731–1788).

In hand binding, a style with ornaments of a leafy character, with a rather solid face, though lightly shaded by the graver. It is best exemplified in borders. The ornaments are often styled Renaissance, being an entire change from the *Gascon* style (*q.v.*).

descender   That part of a lowercase letter that descends below the small letters such as a, e, o, n, m, etc. as in g, j, p, q, y. *See also* ascender.

desiderata   A list of books wanted.

design   (1) To plan a book's entire graphic format. (2) The specifications for the graphic format of a book.

De Vinne, Theodore L. (1828–1914)   New York printer of distinguished output. Authority on printing history and practice, printer of the *Century Magazine*, a founder of the Grolier Club, and the author of several books on printing and typography, including *The Invention of Printing* (1876).

Dewey, Melvil (1851–1931)   Originator of the decimal system of classification which bears his name. Founder of the first school for training
librarians; co-founder, with Frederick Leypoldt and R. R. Bowker, of the
Library Journal, and its first editor; one of the founders of the American
Library Association, and for many years its secretary and then president.
Dewey was an advocate of spelling reform, and used his system in his own
writings.

Dewey decimal classification   A system, often referred to as D.C., of
classifying books on a decimal basis, devised by Melvil Dewey in 1876. The
main classifications, preceding the decimal point, are:

000 **General Works**	400 **Language**	700 **The Arts**
100 **Philosophy**	500 **Pure Science**	800 **Literature**
200 **Religion**	600 **Technology**	900 **History**
300 **Social Sciences**		

The system is used in many libraries throughout the world as a means of
grouping books upon the shelves. In some places, notably Great Britain, it is
also the basis of the subject section of the card catalog. *See also* Library of
Congress classification.

diaper   In bookbinding, a small pattern or ornament repeated in a regular
all-over design.

diazo   A relatively slow-reacting light-sensitive process in which materials
containing azo dyes are exposed to strong blue and ultraviolet light through
photographic negatives or positives to form images. Diazo materials are
developed by ammonia vapor or alkaline solution, and are widely used for
photocomposition proofs.

Dibdin, Thomas Frognall (1776–1847)   English bibliographer. Ordained a
clergyman in 1804. The first of his bibliographical works was his *Introduction
to the Knowledge of Editions of the Classics* (1802), which brought him under the
notice of the third Earl Spencer, who opened to him the rich library at
Althorp, described by Dibdin in *Bibliotheca Spenceriana* (4 vols., 1814–15), and
three additional volumes issued in 1822–23. Among the most popular of his
discursive works about books were *The Bibliomania, or Book-Madness* (1809);
The Bibliographical Decameron (3 vols., 1817); and *A Bibliographical, Antiquarian
... Tour in France & Germany* (3 vols., 1821).

Dibdin was the originator and vice-president (Lord Spencer being the
president) of the Roxburghe Club, founded in 1812. This was the first of
numerous book clubs which have done much service to literature, and to this
day is still the most prestigious.

diced calf or morocco   Binding with cross lined tooling resembling dice or
small squares.

dictionary (in computerized typesetting)   *See* exception dictionary.

dictionary catalog   A catalog in which all entries (e.g., subject, title, author) are arranged in a single alphabetical sequence (as opposed to a classified catalog).

Didot   A family name notable in French printing and publishing. Francois Didot (1689–1757) founded the firm of Didot, in Paris, in 1713, and many of his descendants were associated with type founding, printing, or publishing. His grandson, Firmin Didot (1764–1836), continued the firm, which is still in existence today. Firmin Didot was a printer, engraver, and type founder, whose use of stereotyping revolutionized the making of cheap editions.

die   *See* binder's dies.

die-cutting   Cutting of odd-shaped areas out of a sheet of paper through use of a specially shaped die. Done on either a regular printing press or a special cutting and creasing press by impressing a raised die into the paper.

digital computer   A computer which handles data in discrete, countable units, as opposed to an analog computer which measures differentials continuously. *See also* analog computer.

digital plotter   A computer output device used to draw graphic images on paper under the control of digital signals.

digitizer   A device which converts data into discrete, countable digits or bits.

dime novel   A term covering a type of paper-covered fiction popular during the latter half of the nineteenth century.

direct-impression   A form of composition created by the striking of the image onto the carrier surface, by physical impact of a raised type character against an inked ribbon which in turn is pressed against a substrate such as paper. Typewriter composition is the most prevalent form of direct-impression composition. *See also* cold type; struck-image.

direct mail   Advertising material mailed to lists of prospective purchasers in order to solicit orders.

disc   In photographic typesetting, a circular carrier containing master character images which are used to project characters onto photographic materials. A number of phototypesetting machines use the disc principle.

discount   In the book trade, a percentage from the list (retail selling) price of a book, designated to determine the cost of the book to the dealer in purchasing it from the publisher or wholesaler. Thus, a ten-dollar book sold to a dealer at forty percent discount costs him six dollars, and from this forty percent difference he pays all his operating costs and obtains his profit. *Trade discounts*, variously scaled upwards from thirty to forty percent, forty-five percent and upward (depending on the individual publisher and quantities purchased) are discounts established for selling to wholesalers and retailers. *Short discounts* are lower discounts, offered on the relatively few retail sales of books ordinarily sold directly to professional persons or institutions. *Library discounts* are special discounts offered to library purchasers. *Professional* or *courtesy discounts* are those offered to individuals. *Cash discounts* (for example, two percent off the total of a bill if it is paid in thirty days or less) are those offered for prompt payment of an invoice. *See also* markup.

discretionary hyphen A special hyphenation code placed in a word which the computer can use if it needs to break the word at that point to end a line, but which it also can ignore and discard from the final typeset product if the word does not fall at the end of a line.

disk pack In a computer system, a grouping of magnetic disks, similar in appearance to phonograph records, which are used to store data. Disk packs offer very large storage capacities and random access to the stored data. *See also* magnetic storage; random access storage.

display tube Synonym for video display tube.

display type A general term meaning the larger or heavier typefaces designed for headings, advertisements, etc., as distinguished from text type or body type.

dividend An extra book or books supplied by a book club to the subscriber who has purchased a given number, or has recruited a new subscriber.

divinity circuit Flexible binding, usually of soft leather, as seal or levant, with extended edges that bend over the body of the book. Used principally for Bibles and prayer books, and sometimes on small secular books for pocket use. Known also as *circuit edges*. Originally in circuit edges the four corners of the overlapping leather were slit. The English name for this binding is *yapp*.

divisional title A page preceding a section or division of a book, bearing the name or number of the section or division. Verso of the page is usually blank. Also called *part title*.

documentation (1) The systematic collection, classification, recording, storage, and dissemination of specialized information, generally of a technical or scientific nature. (2) Written description of a computerized system's operating programs and facilities. A full and complete documentation is very important to a system's maintenance, and often is the only means of finding out how to change the system when it becomes desirable to do so after its installation.

Dolphin, The A periodical published irregularly between 1933 and 1941 by the Limited Editions Club of New York. It has been considered the American successor to the English *Fleuron*, and was planned "for all people who find pleasure in fine books." Number I appeared in 1933, number II in 1935, and number III ("A History of the Printed Book," ed. by Lawrence C. Wroth) in 1938. Number IV appeared in three parts: Fall 1940, Winter 1940–1941; and Spring 1941.

dos-a-dos-binding Two books bound back to back so that the back cover of one serves as the back cover of the other, with the fore-edges of one next to the spine of the other.

double elephant folio *See* book sizes.

double numeration A system of enumeration often used in technical and textbooks. The number of the chapter is the key number, and illustrations, charts, etc. are numbered on that basis; e.g., Fig. 14.2 indicates the second figure in the fourteenth chapter.

Doubleday, Nelson (1889–1949) Developer of the Doubleday organization as a major, multifaceted enterprise, unprecedented in the book business because of its size and variety. Son of the founder, Frank Nelson Doubleday, Nelson started his own firm in 1910 under the senior firm's wing, and developed imaginative techniques for mail-order selling; founded the reprint subsidiary, Garden City Publishing Co., in 1925; took over the Literary Guild and launched numerous other book clubs, making use of the parent firm's Country Life Press; expanded the Doubleday Book Shops; and encouraged an exemplary level of management expertise.

doublure From the French "doubler," to line. Ornamental lining of a book cover made with tooled leather, silk, or other material.

Doves Press A private press founded in 1900 at Hammersmith, London, by Thomas James Cobden-Sanderson (1840–1922), and Emery Walker (1851–1933), expert typographer, guide and inspiration of William Morris's Kelmscott Press. The idea of the Doves Press originated from Cobden-Sanderson, who was not then a printer, but who was a master bookbinder of renown, and owner of the Doves Bindery. The two men formed a loose partnership, the money for the press being provided by Mrs. Cobden-Sanderson. Walker designed a special type for the Doves Press, based upon the type used by Nicolas Jenson in his edition of Pliny's *Historia Naturalis* printed at Venice in 1476. Walker's "Doves type" was the only font used by the Doves Press in the forty-one works issued during its existence, 1900–

1916. With the exception of the final *Catalogue Raisonne. . . No. III* (1916), none of the works had illustrations, but some, notably *Paradise Lost* (1902) and *The English Bible* (5 vols., 1903–05), had striking initial letters and opening lines on the first pages printed in red from hand-designed letters drawn by the calligrapher Edward Johnston and carved on wood blocks. *The English Bible* was the most ambitious production of the Doves Press, and the only work issued there in folio. Some of the other Doves books were decorated with initial letters and flourishes, in colors, by Edward Johnston, Graily Hewitt, and Ethel Offer.

In 1908 Cobden-Sanderson dissolved his partnership with Walker, and a dispute arose about the Doves type. This dispute was settled, apparently, when both men signed an agreement allowing Cobden-Sanderson the sole use of the type during his lifetime, and that upon the death of either partner the type should revert to the survivor. Despite the agreement, Cobden-Sanderson (who now operated the press alone) decided that no one but himself should ever print with the Doves type. In March 1913 he threw the matrices into the Thames River, and in the autumn of 1916 he threw the type itself into the Thames. It was not until after Cobden-Sanderson's death in 1922 that Walker obtained any form of reparation for the loss of his property. His suit against Cobden-Sanderson's estate was settled privately.

drop folio   A folio number at the bottom of a page.

drop initials   Initial letters aligned with the top of the letters which follow, but extending below into space provided by the indention of the following line or lines.

drop ship   To ship an order to one address (e.g., the customer) while billing it to another (e.g., a retailer).

drum storage   A rotating cylinder with a magnetic surface on which electrical signals can be recorded. *See also* magnetic storage; random access storage.

dry offset   Indirect relief printing; a form of letterpress using shallow-etched plates, rotary presses, and indirect image transfer from the plate by means of a rubber blanket to the paper. The method resembles offset printing but is known as dry because the plates being in relief do not require moistening. Dry offset is used with sheet-fed and roll-fed presses, mainly for various specialties.

dry point   A method of engraving on metal plates with a sharp needle, producing fine lines without acid. *See also* intaglio printing; etching.

dull-coated   A coated paper made without a glossy surface, but smooth enough to take fine halftones.

dummy (1) Unprinted paper, folded, trimmed or untrimmed, bound or unbound, to show size, bulk and general appearance of a protected publication. "Salesmen's dummies" usually have the first sixteen or thirty-two pages printed and sometimes repeated, in order to present the appearance of a completely printed book. (2) Galley proofs trimmed and pasted up into layouts of columns and pages for the printer's guidance in making up the pages in type. To make such a dummy is to "dummy up."

dump To transfer the contents of a computer memory to another location, either another section of memory or to some form of output.

duodecimo (12mo) *See* book sizes.

duotone Process for reproducing an illustration in two colors from plates made from a one-color original to achieve added depth and beauty.

durable paper *See* paper permanence.

dust jacket The paper (or, in some cases, acetate) cover folded over a bound book, not so much to protect the book from dust as to provide printed display and often illustrative material (which sometimes includes biographical information about the author and short critical notices about the book) to enhance the visibility and sale of the book. Hence, the term "dust" used with "jacket" is essentially an archaism, but it has been revived in common usage in the mid-twentieth century. *See also* jacket band.

dust wrapper *See* dust jacket.

duty *See* tariff.

Dwiggins, W. A. (1880–1956) Distinguished American calligrapher, designer of books, type, and decorations, whose book jackets, endpapers, hand-drawn lettering for title pages, and original bindings did much to revive interest in good book trade design. Among the types he designed are the Electra and the Caledonia.

EDP Electronic data processing.

e.o.m. Abbreviation for "end of month."

easy book Library term for a children's book for the youngest readers. Usually primarily illustrative rather than text.

editing Modification of existing text including such functions as adding, deleting, moving, or changing of material. In computer terminology, editing operations also are called "file maintenance" and "updating." *See also* editing terminal; optical character recognition.

editing terminal A computer input/output device which permits the operator to manipulate text within the system by performing basic editing functions. Some terminals also provide formatting functions as well. Terminals are of two general types, the hard-copy type and the video display type. Both kinds have a standard typewriter keyboard with additional special function and code keys ranged around the standard layout. The hard-copy terminal types out material in the computer, as well as instructions given it and the finished results of editing changes, on a typewriter-style unit. The video display terminal shows the text on a television-like cathode-ray tube screen, and changes made in the text are shown instantly on the video screen. *See also* editing; formatting; hard copy; video display terminal; optical character recognition.

editio princeps   Latin for "first edition." (1) First printed edition of a work which existed in manuscript before printing was invented. (2) Sometimes extended to include the first edition of any work newly printed, but for this last meaning the term "first edition" is preferred.

edition   (1) One of the differing forms in which a literary work or collection of works is published, e.g., as applied to text, original, revised, enlarged, corrected, etc., either by the author himself or by a subsequent editor; as applied to format: de luxe, library, paperbound, large-paper, illustrated, etc. (2) Gaskell, *A New Introduction to Bibliography*, 1972, says, in referring to modern books, "An *edition*, first of all, is all the copies of a book printed at any time (or times) from substantially the same setting of type, and includes all the various impressions, issues, and states which may have been derived from that setting. As to the meaning of 'substantially the same setting of type,' there are bound to be ambiguous cases, but we may take it as a simple rule of thumb that there is a new edition when more than half the type has been reset, but that if less than half the type has been reset we are probably dealing with another impression, issue, or state."* *See also* new edition; issue; impression; state.

edition binding   *See* binding.

editor   (1) The person in charge of selecting and organizing material to be published. (2) One who prepares for publication a work or collection of works not his own. The editorial labor may be: the revision or elucidation of the text and the addition of introductions, notes, and other critical matter; or it may be limited to the preparation of the matter for the printer, and the checking of fact. On the other hand, it may involve the seeking out of a suitable author to realize an editorial idea; encouraging an author to develop an idea or manuscript he or she has submitted, and offering

*Gaskell, Philip. *A New Introduction to Bibliography*. © 1972 Oxford University Press. Reproduced by permission of The Clarendon Press, Oxford.

continuous constructive criticism to help turn it into a publishable book; bargaining with authors' agents; arriving at contract terms; organizing a group of other editors to carry out a complex editorial project; tailoring an editorial plan to meet market and subsidiary possibilities. Editorial departments in major houses are often organized according to these and other functions to be filled. (3) An administrator of an editorial department, e.g., a managing editor.

editorial copies   *See* review copies.

educational materials   *See* book.

Edwards of Halifax   *See* fore-edge painting.

eggshell   A finish on uncoated paper presenting a nonglossy, soft, smooth effect. Most antique paper has an eggshell finish.

electronic character matrix   In cathode-ray tube phototypesetters, the layout of electronic data that describes the image of type characters digitally stored in memory. This data is used to construct characters on the CRT face by drawing lines of light of varying length and spacing.

electronic data processing   Data processing done with electronic systems. *See also* data processing.

electrostatics   The science of static electricity, principles of which are used in xerography and other forms of electrostatic printing. In such printing systems, electrical charges are placed on the sheet to be printed in the image areas, and ink particles are attracted to the image areas by these charges. Then the ink is fused permanently in position. Electrostatics are widely used in photocopying systems and computer printout devices.

electrotype plates; electros   Duplicate plates for letterpress, capable of combining type and pictures in highest quality, suitable for very long production runs. Can be made flat or curved to be used on any kind of letterpress equipment. The making of electros is a complex process requiring molding of the material, electro-deposition of copper in the mold, casting of metal in the copper shell, finishing, and plating, to mention some.

Electros are still being used in book manufacturing, particularly for long runs, but the great advances in web-offset lithography are reducing their importance in the book industry.

elephant folio   *See* book sizes.

elhi   Abbreviation for textbooks published for the elementary school and high school market.

Eliot, John (1604–1690) Colonial clergyman, known as the "Apostle to the Indians." He migrated to Massachusetts in 1631 and settled first in Boston. In the fall of 1632 he became "teacher" to the Church at Roxbury, and he served there in that post until his death. From his first sight of the Indians he was inspired with the idea of converting them. He studied the Indian language, and in 1654 he published his *Primer of the Massachusetts Indian Language* (a vanished Cambridge imprint), and in 1664 he completed his *Indian Grammar Begun*. In addition to his various translations of religious works into the Indian language, his literary activities included tracts and reports, and he was, with Richard Mather, one of the editors of the *Bay Psalm Book* (1640).

Eliot's translation of the Bible into the Massachusetts dialect of the Algonquian Indian language was printed at Cambridge, Massachusetts, by Samuel Green and Marmaduke Johnson; the New Testament appeared in 1661 and the Old Testament in 1663. John Eliot's Bible in the Indian language has the distinction of being the first printing of the Scriptures in the New World.

elite Elite type is the smaller of the two common styles of typewriter type, having twelve characters per inch as against ten for the larger "pica" size.

Elzevir A family of Dutch printers and booksellers. The business was founded in Leyden, in 1583, by Louis Elzevir (1542–1617), and five of his seven sons followed the profession. The firm was best known for its Latin reprints of the classics in pocket-sized editions. Other Elzevirs continued the business until 1791.

em The em is in America the unit for measuring the area of composition. The em is the square of the body of any type. Thus the em of ten-point type is ten points square, the em of twelve-point type is twelve points square, and so on.

An em is so called because the letter M was usually cast on a square body. It is common to specify paragraph indentions of 1-em, or 2-em, etc. *See also* en.

embossed Printed or stamped with dies of letters or a design, on paper, cloth, leather, etc., so that the surface of the sheet of material is left with a bas-relief impression of the image.

embroidered binding Binding ornamented with needlework design in thread or metal.

en One-half the width of an em in type measurement. *See also* em.

enamel A form of *coated paper* (*q.v.*).

encode to translate data into a code, such as the keyboarding of alphanumeric characters and operating instructions into machine-language codes.

endpapers Paper, white or colored, printed or unprinted, placed at the beginning and end of a book, one-half pasted to the inside of the cover, and the fold being bound to the rest of the pages. Endpapers fasten the book to its cover, and are not generally included in a book's pagination. Also called *lining papers* and *paste-downs*.

English finish A calendered paper, smooth but without gloss. *See also* calendering.

engravers' proofs *See* proofs.

engraving (1) A halftone or line cut. (2) The printed reproduction from such a cut. (3) The act of making an engraving. (4) An intaglio plate. *See* copperplate engraving.

   Properly speaking, an engraving is a plate prepared by incising the design into the surface with a graver or burin. Copper and steel engravings are true engravings. Photoengravings are actually produced by etching, not by engraving.

   In the earliest years of printing, illustrations for books were cut in wood. Before the end of the fifteenth century, copper engraved plates came into use and had by the last decade of the sixteenth century essentially changed bookmaking all over Europe. They eventually replaced the woodcut, except for head-pieces, tail-pieces, and decorative initials. Copper was followed by steel in the mid-nineteenth century as the popular medium, then by a revival of wood, then by the photographic processes.

ephemera Material of transitory interest or value; generally pamphlets or clippings.

Ephrata A town in the interior of Pennsylvania where printing was carried on from 1745 to 1820. The Ephrata Press was the second German Press established in Pennsylvania. It was founded by the Seventh Day Baptist Brotherhood at Ephrata. Many publications were issued, among them, the largest work (1,514 pages in folio) printed in America in colonial times, *Der Blutige Schau Platz*, or, *Book of Martyrs* (1748).

erase To remove data from memory without leaving a record of it. In a computer, erasing is the equivalent of clearing. In a display device, it is to remove the image from the viewing screen. *See also* clear.

erotica In cataloging, amatory books. Technically, erotica are legal; pornographica forbidden; but the distinction is often blurred in the U.S. *See also* curiosa; facetiae; pornography.

errata (*sing.* **erratum**) Errors discovered in a book after printing. Corrections of these errors are usually printed on a slip or a page and pasted or laid into the volume. In some books errata may be found printed almost anywhere in the text. Also called *corrigenda.*

error rate The ratio of lines with errors in them to total lines, or error words to total words, or error keystrokes to total keystrokes.

esparto A coarse grass grown in Spain and other Mediterranean countries, used extensively in England for papermaking.

Estienne Name of a distinguished French printing family of the sixteenth century. The firm was founded in 1501 by Henri Estienne, sometimes called Henri I, to distinguish him from his grandson, Henry II (1528–98). Under the guidance of Simon de Colines (*q.v.*), his successor, and later of his son, Robert Estienne (1503–59) the second of his three sons, the firm led the French printing renaissance, popularizing roman and italic types, and making available inexpensive editions of the classics.

Robert Estienne became printer to Francis I, but later moved to Geneva because of his identification with the reformation movement. Noted for scholarship as well as for printing, Robert compiled the first modern French-Latin dictionary.

Robert's son, Henri, who succeeded to the business, also edited and printed many editions of the Greek and Latin classics.

The name "Estienne" was Latinized, Stephanus; Anglicized, Stephens — both so listed in some works of reference.

etching (1) A print from a plate into which the design has been etched (eaten) by acid. (A "dry point" etching is thus not a true etching.) (2) The process of preparing such a plate.

Evans, Charles (1850–1935) Librarian, and bibliographer, born in Boston in 1850, died in Chicago 8 February 1935. His fame rests on his monumental historical-bibliographical compilation, *American Bibliography, a Chronological Dictionary of All Books, Pamphlets, and Periodical Publications Printed in the United States, from the Genesis of Printing in 1639 down to and including the Year 1820. . .* which during his lifetime he completed through the letter "M" of the year 1799 (Volumes I–XII, printed 1903–34).

The latter part of the year 1799 and the whole of the year 1800 was completed by Clifford K. Shipton of the American Antiquarian Society, and his work came out as Volume XIII of Evans, printed in 1955. Volume XIV, an author-title-subject Index to Evans, by Roger P. Bristol, was added in

1959. Bristol also compiled an Index of Printers, Publishers, and Booksellers listed in Evans, issued in 1961; and, a preliminary checking edition of a Supplement to include titles not found in Evans, issued in 1962.

The period between 1800, when Evans stops, and 1820, when Roorbach starts, is covered by a preliminary checklist "gathered entirely from secondary sources" (admittedly designed as a first step) by Ralph R. Shaw and Richard H. Shoemaker, *American Bibliography: A Preliminary Check-list. . . 1801–1819,* and Addenda volume. Together 20 volumes, New York, Scarecrow Press, 1958–1965.

Eve   Nicolas and Clovis Eve, both of whom bore the title of Binder to the King of France, the first under Henri III, and the second under Henri IV and Louis XIII. Clovis was probably son or nephew of Nicolas, and according to an old authority, he invented marbled paper. The name Eve is associated with an elaborate style of hand binding used at the end of the sixteenth and beginning of the seventeenth centuries.

EX   (1) Invoice symbol meaning "see explanation herewith." (2) Also an abbreviation for "full exchange on returns."

ex-height   Term used in describing type images. (By some also known as zee-height.) The height of most lowercase letters such as a, c, e, m, o, s, for example. Some lowercase letters extend above, some below their ex-height. *See also* ascenders and descenders.

Ex-height, ascender, and descender. From *Printing Industry*, p. 56, col. 2.

ex libris   Latin phrase frequently used on bookplates, and coupled with the owner's name, in which case it means "from the library of" that person. Sometimes used as a synonym for the word *bookplate.*

exception dictionary   In computerized typesetting, a collection of common recurring words which do not hyphenate according to standard rules in the computer's hyphenation program. These exception words are stored in memory with their correct hyphenations, and the computer looks up the proper hyphenations when needed.

execute   To perform an instruction or set of instructions on data, both of which were given to the computer prior to the order to execute.

export edition   An edition of a book supplied to a foreign market, in sheets or bound, usually at less than the normal wholesale rate and at a lower rate of royalty.

export representative   An organization handling the promotion and sale of a publisher's books outside the country of origin. The contract usually calls for a commission on sales. In addition, the publisher often shares the cost of promotion in the export market.

expurgated   An edition of a work from which certain original material considered objectionable has been removed.

external storage   A facility outside of the computer's central processing unit in which additional data can be stored and drawn on as needed.

extra binding   A hand binding of more than usual elegance.

extra-illustrated   Illustrated by extra matter added to and bound into a volume or set. This added material usually consists of engravings, letters, or documents referred to in the text. These are mounted, inlaid, or trimmed to fit the size of the books in which they are inserted.

Sometimes called *grangerized*, because James Granger's *Biographical History of England* was a favorite choice for such treatment.

Fabriano paper   An Italian paper used in fine and special editions, made by an Italian paper mill founded in about 1270 and still flourishing.

face   A style of type.

facetiae   Coarsely witty books; objectionable or indecent works collectively. *See also* curiosa; erotica; pornography.

facsimile edition   An exact reproduction of an original work, often printed by photogelatin lithography or gravure.

facsimile transmission   The sending of a graphic or pictorial copy over communications links such as telephone lines. A sending unit at one end of the line translates the visual image into a series of electrical signals, which are received at the other end and used to operate a transcription device which reproduces the visual image on paper or photographic material.

fair trade   A legal device first enacted in the 1930s to prevent cut-price competition on branded merchandise, such as drugs, appliances, books, etc. State fair trade laws permit manufacturers or publishers, by agreement with retailers, to establish minimum resale prices for specific goods. A federal law authorizes such contracts in interstate commerce. A contract with a single retailer in a state is binding upon all dealers in that state.

fair use   A use of copyrighted material without express authorization of the copyright owner but permitted, although not specifically defined in law. Generally, fair use must meet several criteria: the use should not impair the value of the copyright by copying so much of the copyrighted material as to diminish demand for it; the copier should not have used the copyright owner's efforts as a substitute for his own intellectual labor; the use should be "fair" as a reasonable person would view it, not unjust or damaging to the original. The principle of fair use has been heavily in litigation, as in the case between the publisher Williams & Wilkins and several public institutions which have felt they could fairly make extensive xerographic copies from the publisher's medical journals.

fat matter   In printing, copy for composition that can be more readily set than the average. In contradistinction, *lean matter* requires full average time, or more. *See also* matter.

fax   Abbreviation for facsimile.

featherweight   A term applied to printing paper, light in weight, but thick in bulk.

Fell types   Between 1667 and 1672 Dr. John Fell imported from Holland some fine types which he presented to Oxford University. From these were cut fonts that gave a new impulse to English type design. The original fonts are still in use at the Clarendon Press.

field   A group of related characters treated as a unit in computer operations, particularly in setting up storage or file schemes for various purposes.

file maintenance   The activity of keeping a computer file up to date by adding, deleting, moving, or changing data in it. *See also* editing.

fillet   (1) An ornamental line, plain or of repetitive design, usually of gold, impressed on the cover of a book. (2) The stamp or wheeled tool for making the above.

filmsetting   Typesetting on film. Sometimes used interchangeably with phototypesetting, but incorrectly as phototypesetting also includes material set on light-sensitive paper. *See also* phototypesetting.

finishing   A bookbinder's term for the completion of binding after the book has passed through the forwarding (*q.v.*) operations. In hand binding, finishing includes the polishing of the leather, its ornamentation and lettering. Finishing is also used (as in "mounting and finishing") to cover such specialty binding operations as die-cutting, eye-letting, stringing, tin-edging, etc.

first-choice hyphenation   The first choice for hyphenating a word as specified in *Webster's Eighth New Collegiate Dictionary*, the reference most used for computer hyphenation programs. *See also* hyphenation.

first edition   (1) The whole number of copies first printed from the same type and issued at the same time. (2) The text of a book in its original form as first published. (3) In bibliography first edition is the same as (1) above with certain refinements pertaining to *issue* (*q.v.*) and *state* (*q.v.*).

firsts First editions.

flag A special code used at the beginning or end of data requiring some type of special treatment, signaling some kind of change in condition.

flat The sheet containing offset negatives or positives in the proper arrangement, from which the printing plate is made.

flat back A binding on which the back is not rounded.

flat-bed cylinder press Letterpresses of different designs having a flat bed containing the type form and a rotating impression cylinder carrying the paper. Such presses are made as single-color, two-color, and perfecting presses which print both side of the sheet in a single pass.

  Flat-bed cylinder presses used to be the workhorses of book printing; they are increasingly being superseded by offset lithographic presses. American press builders discontinued the making of these presses during the 1960s. European press manufacturers are exporting various kinds into this country.

flat display A display of books featuring the front covers rather than the spines of the books.

Fleuron, The An annual on typography conducted in London for seven years (1923–1930) under the editorship of Oliver Simon and Stanley Morison. The distinguished and scholarly character of its contributions had an important effect on the art of printing.

flexible binding A binding in which the boards are flexible rather than stiff. *See also* limp binding.

floor In bidding for paperback reprint or other rights to a book or manuscript, a first serious offer.

Florence Agreement (Agreement on the Importation of Educational, Scientific, and Cultural Materials) A UNESCO-sponsored international agreement which eliminates tariffs, discriminatory taxation and, to some extent, other trade barriers on a wide range of published materials, art objects, antiques, and scientific apparatus, plus audiovisual materials with an educational, scientific, and cultural character, imported by approved institutions. Drafted in 1950, the Agreement was ratified by the United States in 1967; by 1973, sixty-eight countries were members. Liberalizing additions to the Florence Agreement were recommended at a conference in Geneva in 1973 called to review the Florence Agreement and the related Beirut Agreement (*q.v.*).

floret; flower An ornament in the shape of a small flower or leaf, used in binding or printing. Sometimes called *printer's flower*.

flowchart   A graphic diagram of all functions and sequences involved in the flow of work from start to finish of an operation. It is used in the analysis, planning, and documentation of computer operations and systems.

flush   "Even with." Usually interpreted as meaning even with left margin, unless otherwise designated. *See also* cut flush.

fly title   *See* bastard title.

flyleaf   Binder's blank leaf, following the free front endpaper. Often used, inaccurately, to describe the free front endpaper itself.

foil   Tissue-thin material, faced with metal or pigment, used in book stamping. A heated die impresses the foil onto the cover material, causing the metal or pigment to transfer to the cover.

folding (folded) plate   An illustration which has to be folded to fit into the bound book.

foliation   The numbering of the physical leaves or sheets in a book rather than the pages which are printed on both sides of the leaves.

folio   A leaf numbered on the recto; the numeral itself in a book or manuscript in which the leaves are numbered. *See also* book sizes.

follow copy   In typesetting and proofreading: an order to set up matter exactly as it appears in copy, making no changes whatever in spelling, punctuation, capitalization, etc. Horace Greeley's famous injunction to his compositors was to "follow copy even if it goes out of the window."

font   From the French "fondre," to cast. A complete assortment of types of one face and size. A complete font includes capitals, small capitals, lower-case letters, numerals, punctuation marks, ligatures, etc.

foolscap   A sheet of paper about 13 × 16 inches, making when folded a page size 13 × 8 inches. The name is derived from the watermark of a fool's cap and bells used by old papermakers. *See also* book sizes.

foolscap folio; foolscap octavo; foolscap quarto   *See* book sizes.

foot   The end or bottom of a page. *See also* head.

footnote   A note at the foot of a page, usually in smaller type than the text, giving a reference, an authority, or an elucidation of matter in text. *See also* reference marks; marginalia.

fore-edge   The front edge of a book, opposite its spine.

fore-edge painting   A picture painted on the fore-edges of the leaves of a book, over which gold is usually applied. The picture is not visible when the volume is closed, but can be seen by fanning the leaves open obliquely. The "double fore-edge" contains two paintings which can be seen singly by fanning the leaves first one way, then the reverse. A "triple fore-edge" contains two hidden paintings and one visible painting.

The technique of the hidden painting, or paintings, on the fore-edges of the leaves of a book was originated in the middle seventeenth century in England. It was revived in the latter half of the eighteenth century in England by Edwards of Halifax—the family of bookbinders (William Edwards and his five sons) who operated in the Edwards's hometown of Halifax and in London. William Edwards (1723–1808) is more particularly associated with the fore-edge paintings produced by the various Edwards shops; the technique was continued with great success by his son Thomas, who worked in the Halifax shop until 1826. Three other sons, James, John, and Richard, worked in other Edwards shops in London.

Fore-edge paintings were also produced by other binders of the period, among them the most notable being Kalthoeber, one of five German binders of the late eighteenth century working in London.

foreword Prefatory or introductory remarks to a book by someone other than the author. *See also* preface; introduction.

form In printing a "form" is any assembly of pages that can be printed simultaneously in a single "impression" of the printing press. In letterpress, the word may refer either to the physical metal type or plates as locked up in a *chase* ready for press, or to the selection of pages involved. In offset, the work is usually employed only in the latter sense (e.g., "A paper jam occurred toward the end of the run on the third form.")

In book printing, a form is likely to consist of 16 or 32 pages, depending on the size of the press, but 24s, 48s, and 64s are not uncommon and 4s, 8s, and 12s do occur. In English usage the word is spelled *forme*.

form entry An entry in an index or catalog which lists books according to (1) the form in which their subject material is organized, such as "Directories" or "Periodicals"; or (2) their literary form, such as "Poetry" or "Addresses, essays, lectures."

form heading A heading used for a form entry (*q.v.*) in an index or catalog.

format The graphic and physical makeup of a book as to size, type page, margins, binding, etc.

format instruction code A special character code used to distinguish between alphanumeric codes and instruction or function codes. Because most keyboards and display devices are limited in the number of different characters they can handle, a special instruction code (such as a $ or #) is inserted just prior to an instruction to tell the machine that what follows is an instruction, not actual text or data. Then standard alphanumeric codes are given a new set of meanings for instruction purposes. When the instruction is completed, a second format instruction code is inserted to tell the computer that what follows is now text or data. *See also* function code; instruction.

format storage   The storage of format specifications in computer memory for withdrawal and use on command from a special code. *See also* macro code.

formatting   The insertion of typeface, size, spacing, indention, run-around, or other typographic instructions to direct the typesetting machine to set material in the selected typefaces and in proper position in an area. Formatting can be of two types: galley formatting in which type is produced in columnar format, and page formatting in which type is positioned within the page area. *See also* editing.

fortyeightmo (48mo)   *See* book sizes.

forwarding   The intermediate steps in binding: rounding and backing or lining. These occur after *sewing* and prior to the *finishing* operations. Sometimes included under forwarding are such auxiliary operations as tipping-in, pasting on endpapers, etc. In hand binding, a somewhat different grouping of operations comes under forwarding, including insertion of plates, sewing, tying in of boards and covering. *See also* sewing; finishing.

Fotosetter   The first of the successful phototypesetters, introduced by Intertype, and closely resembling an Intertype hot-metal typesetter, except that it produces lines of type photographically on film or paper. The Fotosetter is a photomechanical machine and was superseded by more technologically advanced systems, developed by Intertype and other companies.

foundry proofs   *See* proofs.

foundry type   Type cast for hand composition, and sold in fonts.

fount   British term for *font (q.v.)*.

four-color process   *See* process color.

Fourdrinier   Machine for making paper in an endless web, introduced by Henry and Sealy Fourdrinier early in the nineteenth century. Pulp in liquid form is flowed onto a moving wire screen where most of the water drains out. The web then passes through a series of rollers which complete the drying process and impart the desired finish.

Fournier, Pierre Simon (le jeune)   (1712–1768)   French engraver and type founder, who wrote several important works relating to typography. His principal work was the *Manuel Typographique* (2 vols. 1764), the first volume treating of engraving and type founding, the second of printing, with examples of different alphabets. With an older brother, Jean Pierre, he succeeded to the foundry of his father, Jean Claude.

foxing A discoloration of brown paper; rust. Stains caused by chemical or metallic impurities in the paper.

fraktur (1) The group name of German blackface type. (2) A type of Pennsylvania Dutch lettering. *See also* antiqua.

Franklin, Benjamin (1706–1790) Printer and publisher, diplomat, statesman, and scientist. Born in Boston, died in Philadelphia. Apprenticed in 1718 to his brother James (1697–1735), printer; after disagreements with James, left Boston (1723). Settled in Philadelphia where he obtained employment as printer. He became proprietor of a printing business and publisher of *The Pennsylvania Gazette* (1730–1748). He served as official printer to Pennsylvania, New Jersey, and Delaware. He was the author-printer-publisher of the *Poor Richard* almanacs for the years 1733–1758, issued under the pseudonym "Richard Saunders." The annual sale of these almanacs averaged 10,000 copies, far exceeding the sale of any other publication in the colonies. He considered his typographical masterpiece to be *M.T. Cicero's Cato Major, or His Discourse of Old Age*, in the translation of James Logan, Chief Justice of the Pennsylvania Supreme Court. The work was issued in 1744.

In 1748 Franklin sold his press to his foreman, and ostensibly retired from full activity in the printing business. However, in the same year he formed a partnership with David Hall, whom he had engaged five years before, and the firm operated as "Franklin & Hall" until 1766, under the management of Hall. The output of Franklin's press from 1729 to 1766 as listed in Dr. William J. Campbell's catalog of *The Collection of Franklin Imprints in the Museum of the Curtis Publishing Company* (1918) comes to 728 entries. This does not include newspapers, paper currency, etc.

After 1748 Franklin devoted most of his time to scientific experiments, and to public life. In 1776 he was sent by Congress as one of a committee of three to negotiate a treaty with France; in 1778 he was appointed sole plenipotentiary, and remained in France until 1785. During his long stay there he established a little private press for his own amusement at his home in Passy, then a suburb of Paris. The history of the Passy press is told by Luther S. Livingston in *Franklin and His Press at Passy* (New York: Grolier Club 1914). Livingston lists thirty-two entries (often referred to as "bagatelles," a term meant to include everything printed by Franklin at his Passy press). Will Ransom's *Private Presses and Their Books* (New York: Bowker, 1929) lists six additional pieces that came to light after 1914.

Franklin established in Philadelphia in 1731 one of the earliest circulating libraries in America (sometimes said to be the earliest), which developed into what is now the Library Company of Philadelphia, and he was one of the founders of the American Philosophical Society (1743). Accounts of his work in public life, and his work as a writer, as a scientist, etc., are outside the scope of this entry.

free sheet   Paper made of *chemical pulp* (*q.v.*) without any admixture of groundwood.

French fold   A sheet printed on one side only and folded into quarters without cutting the fold along the top edge.

French Revolutionary Calendar   *See* calendar.

frisket   Originally part of the hand press, consisting of a light metal frame with a paper stencil stretched over it. Windows were cut in the frisket in printing areas where type would contact the paper. The frisket was placed over the inked type form and the paper was laid over it. When the impression was made, the frisket protected the paper from unwanted ink transfer in nonprinting areas. Today, in the commercial art field, special frisket material is used for making protective stencils for art work.

front matter   The pages preceding the text of a book. According to the best usage these should be arranged in the following order: *Bastard Title* or *Half Title; Frontispiece; Title Page* (with imprint and date of printing); *Copyright Page* (with country where printed and number of printings if more than one); *Dedication; Table of Contents; List of Illustrations; Foreword; Preface; Introduction; Half title* repeated (optional).

Each should begin on a right-hand or odd-numbered page, excepting the *frontispiece* (which faces the title page) and the *copyright page* (which appears on the verso of the title page).

If a list of books by the same author, or other books in the same series, is to be inserted, it is printed on the verso of the bastard title or half title.

frontispiece (front.; frontis.)   An illustration facing the title page.

fugitive material   Printed matter of fleeting interest, produced in limited quantities, such as a program printed for a certain occasion.

full binding   *See* binding.

full measure   Extending across the whole width of a type column.

function code   A computer code which controls machine operations, as opposed to a code representing an actual typographic character. *See also* instruction.

furniture   In letterpress, the wooden or metal spacing material which separates type pages or fills space between type and *chase* (*q.v.*).

Fust, Johann (d.1466)   Early German printer. There is no evidence that, as is commonly asserted, Johann Fust was a goldsmith, but he appears to have been a moneylender or banker. Fust became interested in Johann Gutenberg's experiments in printing, and lent him 800 guilders in 1450 and another 800 guilders in 1452, the only security being that of "tools" still to be made. In 1455 Fust brought suit to recover the money he had lent, and on the sixth of November the suit was decided in his favor (*see* Gutenberg). He then took possession of the printing plant and equipment, and also took into service Peter Schoeffer (1425?–1502), a former scriptor who had been employed by Gutenberg as a typesetter and probably as foreman of the plant. Schoeffer married Fust's daughter Dyna at about this time.

The first known publication of the Fust and Schoeffer office was the *Mainz Psalter* of 1457. The book is the first to give date of printing and the names of its printers. Two separate editions were produced in 1457, one with 143 leaves and another with 175 leaves; ten copies are known today, nine of the former and one of the latter, all printed on vellum. The work is remarkable for the beauty of the very large initial letters, each printed in red and blue. The most ambitious publication of the two printers was the great forty-eight-line Bible, printed in two volumes in 1462. The main text was printed in black with small type; the headings and initial letters in large type were printed in red.

After Fust's death in 1466 the business was continued by Schoeffer, who was recognized always as an excellent printer. He died in 1502, after producing fifty-nine separate works as an independent. In 1470 he issued what is believed to be the first bookseller's advertisement of printed books; it was in poster form, and since it contained a line of type quoted from one of his books, it can also be described as the first type specimen sheet.

g.e.   Gilt edges (*q.v.*).

g.t.   Gilt top. *See* gilt edges.

galley proofs; galleys   Proofs taken from type before it has been arranged in page format. Each proof shows the contents of one column of type. The term came originally from hot metal typesetting where newly set type was stored in long shallow trays called galleys which were just wide enough to hold one column of type about 22 inches long. *See also* proofs.

Garamond, Claude (d.1561)   One of the most distinguished of early French type designers. He was a pupil of Geoffroy Tory (*q.v.*). His famous *Grecs du Roi*, three Greek types based upon the handwriting of the calligrapher Angelos Vergetios, were completed in about 1541, and became models for future designers. His roman and italic types were also great success, and brought about the decline in the use of the gothic letter. The roman and italic fonts have been revived and put to much use in the present century.

garbage   Unwanted or useless data in a computer system, or in the output of a system. The initials GIGO express a maxim in the computer field— garbage in, garbage out—which indicates the importance of putting the correct material into a system in the first place.

Gascon, Le   A leading French bookbinder of the seventeenth century whose identity has not been established. His style is distinguished by the dotted face of the ornaments on his bindings instead of the continuous or solid line.

gatefold   A folded illustration or other insert which is larger than the publication into which it is bound, so that it must be unfolded for proper viewing. A gatefold opens out horizontally to the left or right.

gathering   (1) In binding, assembling the signatures of a book in the order in which they are to be bound. (2) In bibliography, used synonymously for *signature* (*q.v.*).

gathering plan   *See* blanket order.

gauffered edges   *See* goffered edges.

gelatin print   *See* photogelatin.

general-purpose computer   A computer designed to be usable for a wide variety of applications, as opposed to a single special purpose. *See also* stored-program computer.

Gesamtkatalog der Wiegendrucke   The great catalog of fifteenth century printed books, edited by a committee of German scholars, with assistance from scholars all over the world. Only volumes I–VII and volume VIII, part one (A-Federicis) have been issued, printed at Leipzig, 1925–1940. The text is in German. As far as published the work is the most comprehensive record of incunabula yet made. The sections published record nearly half again as many editions as Hain's *Repertorium Bibliographicum* (Stuttgart, 1826–38). *See* Hain, Ludwig.

ghost writer   One who writes books or articles for and in the name of another.

giant book   A three-dimensional cardboard blowup of the outside of a book for display purposes.

gift certificate   A certificate sold by retailers and redeemed by them in merchandise in the value stated on the certificate. *See also* Book Token.

Gill, Eric (1882–1940)   Distinguished English artist, illustrator, and designer of types. He made engravings for his own press, St. Dominic, and also for the Golden Cockerel Press (*q.v.*), and type designs such as Perpetua and Gill Sans Serif.

gilt edges   The edges of a book usually trimmed smooth and covered with gold leaf. The abbreviation *g.e.* means gilt edges; *g.t.*, gilt top; *t.e.g.*, top edge gilt.

gilt extra   Binding with more than the usual gilt ornamentation.

glassine   The transparent paper used as a protective book wrapper.

glossy print   A photographic print on a shiny-finished paper. Prints intended for reproduction are usually made on such paper.

gluing off   Process of applying glue to the spine of a book, either after sewing or instead of sewing.

goffered edges   An indented pattern worked with a tool on the edges of the leaves of a book. Also known as *gauffered edges*.

Golden Cockerel Press   English private press founded in 1920 by Harold M. Taylor, for the purpose of making finely produced books available to many at a reasonable cost. Among the eminent artists commissioned to illustrate Golden Cockerel Press books were Eric Gill and Robert Gibbings. The press still publishes, but its books are no longer printed by hand.

Goodhue, Bertram G. (1869–1924)   American architect and designer of type, including the widely popular Cheltenham, and the Merrymount designed for D. B. Updike.

gothic   (1) A style of lettering dating from the twelfth century, the origin of modern black-letter (*q.v.*). (2) A term used by bibliographers to describe black-letter type. (3) In the United States, a common bold type style without serifs. *See also* sans serif. (4) A romantic novel of suspense with a historical and mysterious setting.

Goudy, Frederic W. (1865–1947)   Notable American type designer. Responsible for more than one hundred typefaces, many in general use including the Forum, Kennerley, Goudy, Goudy Open, Hadriano. His wife, Bertha M. Goudy, was a fellow craftsman in their Village Press, Marlborough-on-Hudson, N. Y. His work is described in his own "A Half Century of Type Design and Typography, 1895–1945," published by The Typophiles.

Grabhorn Press   Founded in 1920 by Edwin and Robert Grabhorn, in San Francisco. In its forty-five-year history, the press produced more than 600 books and became known as the greatest American press of this century. The magnificent Grabhorn *Leaves of Grass*, issued in 1930, is considered the finest production of the press, and ranks as one of the great Press Books of the century. In 1965, Edwin, the elder brother, retired for reasons of failing health, and the press was disbanded. The following year Robert Grabhorn and Andrew Hoyem, a young San Francisco printer and poet, who had worked at the Grabhorn Press during 1963–64, formed the Grabhorn-Hoyem Press. Edwin died in 1968. The partnership of Robert Grabhorn and Andrew Hoyem lasted until Robert Grabhorn's death in 1973. Andrew Hoyem continues the direction of the press under his own name.

grain   Direction in a sheet of paper in which most of the fibers lie. In all machine-made paper the fibers which make up the sheet lie to a large degree in one general direction due to the flow of the pulp on the moving screen which forms the sheet. If the grain of a paper runs parallel with the spine of a book, it opens more flexibly. *See also* against the grain.

grangerizing   The extra-illustrating of one work with matter from other sources. James Granger's *Biographical History of England*, published in 1769, lent itself widely to this practice, having had blank pages bound in to receive any desired illustrations. *See also* extra-illustrated.

Granjon, Robert (fl. 1540–1580)   French printer, type designer, and engraver. Designer of the first italics to be used in the modern manner, that is, complementary to roman; one of the first to introduce the use of round notes in musical notation. Among his many type designs he is known especially for his *caractères de civilité*, a typeface based upon cursive French handwriting. He introduced the *Civilité* types at Lyons in about 1557.

graphic arts quality   The print quality obtainable from conventional hot metal or photographic typesetting equipment, as opposed to the quality obtainable from computer printout devices such as chain printers.

graphics   Broadly used, any presentation of data in visual form. Used as opposed to "text" material, any illustrative material such as charts, drawings, art, or any page formatting or area positioning of elements.

graver   *See* burin.

gravure   The major commercial application of the intaglio principle of printing, often used for photographic books and frontispieces. Short-run work is done by sheet-fed gravure; long runs, such as certain national magazines, by rotogravure. The latter is roll-fed and faster. Gravure printing is distinguished by its dense, rich solids, by the unobtrusiveness (almost invisibility) of its screen, and by its ability to print with delicate detail on uncoated paper.

Greenaway Plan *See* blanket order.

Gregorian Calendar *See* calendar.

grid (1) A phototypesetting master carrier of typeface character images from which the machine projects characters onto photographic material. (2) An *x-y* layout of lines over an area for typographic makeup, for location of elements within the area. *See also* coordinate digitizing; grid coordinate system.

grid coordinate system Synonym for coordinate digitizing system. Also used specifically to indicate a method of making corrections in data in computer memory by specifying the line number, and then word number in which the change is to be made, and then designating the actual characters to be changed. *See also* coordinate digitizing; grid.

Grolier, Jean (1479–1565) Famous French patron of the arts of the book, born at Lyons, became treasurer-general of France in 1547. He remains traditionally one of the greatest of all patrons of the binder's art, magnificent leather bindings having been made for him. Many of these bindings were lettered Io. GROLERII ET AMICORUM.

Grolier is the name given to ornamental tooling on hand bindings after his style, i.e., an interlaced framework of geometrical figures—circles, squares, and diamonds—with scrollwork running through it, and ornaments of Moresque character, generally azured in whole or in part, sometimes in outline only.

groove The depression between cover and spine of a binding, formed by the rounding and backing process.

groundwood pulp The raw material from which newsprint and similar papers are made. Groundwood paper has excellent printing quality and opacity but lacks the permanence that is obtainable when the wood fibers are broken down more slowly by chemical rather than mechanical means. *See also* chemical pulp.

Grub Street Described by Dr. Samuel Johnson as "originally the name of a street near Moorfields, much inhabited by writers of small histories, dictionaries, and occasional poems. . . ." The name has been and continues to be associated with literary hacks.

guards (1) Strips of paper or muslin, to which text leaves, illustrations, maps, etc. are attached, and by which they are bound into a volume. (2) Strips of strong paper or cloth used to reinforce the first and last signatures of a book. Also called *hinges.*

guillotine cut   A straight cut in paper made by a guillotine-style cutter blade, as opposed to other types of cuts such as die-cutting, slitting, perforating, etc. The edges of most books are trimmed by guillotine cutting.

Guinzburg, Harold K. (1900–1961)   Publisher and book industry leader. He founded in 1925 the Viking Press, which became known for literary and typographic distinction; he helped found the Literary Guild in 1926. He was a strong influence in establishing the National Book Committee and National Library Week (*q.v.*) and was an exponent of publishers' cooperation in reading development. The Book Committee's National Medal for Literature is supported by a fund set up in his memory.

gussets   *See* buckles.

Gutenberg, Johann (1398?–1468)   Printer at Mainz, Germany, long credited with the invention of printing with movable metal types. Son of the general accountant of the City of Mainz, Frilo Gensfleisch, he adopted the surname of his mother, Elsen Gutenberg, because she was the last of her line and the name would otherwise have become extinct.

He moved to Strassburg in about 1430, where he became known as a maker of mirrors. In 1438 he made an agreement with two helpers to give instruction "*in etlicher kunst*" (in a certain art) which various authorities believe was printing. He returned to Mainz in 1448, and in August 1450 he entered into a partnership with Johann Fust (*q.v.*) who lent him 800 guilders, the security being "tools" still to be made. A further 800 guilders was lent by Fust in 1452. Gutenberg is presumed to have begun printing a large folio Latin Bible, and to have printed during its progress some smaller books and a broadside Papal *Letter of Indulgence* (1454 and 1455).

In 1455 Fust brought suit to recover the monies he had lent. Evidence given in the records of the lawsuit make it clear that Gutenberg was engaged in printing. The suit was decided in Fust's favor, and as Gutenberg was unable to repay the loan, Fust took over the printing plant. He formed a partnership with Gutenberg's foreman, Peter Schoeffer, and it is most likely that the printing of the Bible begun by Gutenberg was finished by Schoeffer before 1456. The work has been known under several names: the *Gutenberg Bible*; the *Mazarin Bible* (so named because the first copy to be given widespread publicity was the copy found in the Mazarin Library at Paris by the bibliographer Francois Guillaume de Bure in 1763); and, in modern times, as the *42-line Bible*, for the number of lines in each printed column. There is no definite proof that the *Gutenberg Bible* was printed entirely by Gutenberg. The work bears no place of printing, no date, and no printer's name.

Little is known about Gutenberg's activities after his break with Fust. In 1465 the Archbishop of Mainz gave him the post of "salaried courtier for life." His name has been, and still is, associated with the printing of the *Catholicon*, a Latin dictionary written by Joannes Balbus in the thirteenth century, and printed at Mainz in 1460. The colophon of the work gives no printer's name, but some experts credit Gutenberg with the printing, and say that it was done with equipment lent to him by Dr. Conrad Humery, of Mainz.

Gutenberg-Jahrbuch   Founded in 1926 by the Gutenberg-Gesellschaft, an international society of those interested in typography, at Mainz. The publication has printed many distinguished contributions on printing and the related arts by scholars of many countries.

gutter   *See* margins.

Hain, Ludwig (1781–1836)   The first bibliographer to make an alphabetical list by author (and where author is unknown, by title) of all incunabula known up to his time. He listed 16,311 books printed before the year 1501 in his *Repertorium Bibliographicum, in quo libri omnes ab arte typographica inventa usque ad annum MD.* . . (2 volumes in 4 volumes, Stuttgart, 1826–1838). A *Supplement.* . . by Walter Arthur Copinger was issued in London, 1895–1902, 2 volumes in 3 volumes. The *Supplement* contains about 7,000 corrections and gives a list of about 6,000 volumes not in Hain.

Hain-Copinger list only about 22,300 editions against the more than 39,000 estimated for the complete *Gesamtkatalog.* . ., but Hain will remain a convenient primary reference work until the *GKW* is completed — if ever it will be. *See* Gesamtkatalog. . . .

hair spaces   Very thin spaces, less than five to an em, used to facilitate the work of letter spacing and justifying the type line.

half-binding   *See* binding.

half-cloth   A binding with a cloth spine and paper-covered sides.

half title   Title just preceding a section of text of a book and occupying a full page. Sometimes used also to refer to the *bastard title* (*q.v.*) *See also* front matter.

halftone   A technique for reproducing by optical illusion the different tonal shadings in photographs, drawings, or paintings. The continuous shadings in the original are broken up photographically into a series of tiny dots almost invisible to the naked eye. The eye, therefore, does not see the individual dots; rather, it perceives an overall tonal effect created by the dots. To create varying tones, these dots vary in diameter in proportion to the lightness or darkness of the tone being reproduced. Smaller dots when printed will cover less area of the sheet with ink while larger dots will coat a larger proportion of the paper with ink. Therefore, smaller dots will present a lighter overall tonal effect to the eye while larger dots will create darker tonal effects. The dots are made on a printing plate by photographing the original through a ruled screen. A screen with very close rulings makes for better details in reproduction but has to be used on a smoother paper. Offset can reproduce much finer screens than letterpress.

hand composition   The division between hand and machine composition is a consequence of the invention of hot metal composition systems in the nineteenth century, resulting in the distinction between machine and hand composition. Hand composition had, and still has, various applications, particularly in advertising.

In book work produced by machine composition, hand composition has a number of functions, including makeup in pages. The photographic and electronic revolution in composition is still too unsettled for generally accepted lines of work division. Some shops still practice traditional hand composition; others use equipment requiring different skills. Page makeup, for example, can be made by paste-up or stripping, in photographic composition, or as part of programming in electronic systems.

handmade paper   Paper made a sheet at a time by dipping up the pulp by hand on to a sieve. The water runs through while the sieve is manipulated in a manner to mix the fibers thoroughly. The pulp is prevented from running over the edge by a thin frame called the deckle. Handmade paper has no grain, is obtainable only in small sizes, and may have deckled edges on all four sides. All paper was so made until the Fourdriniers perfected, about 1800, a machine with a continuous sieve.

hanging indention   A form of typesetting having the first line of a paragraph set to the full width of the measure, while the succeeding lines are indented one or more ems from the left edge. This entry, as all the entries in this book, shows a hanging indention.

hard copy   (1) A typewritten record of material keyboarded into computer coding. (2) A printed (typed or otherwise) record of a computer's output.

hard-wired computer   Synonym for wired-program computer.

hardbound   Bound in cloth- or paper-covered boards. Also called *hard cover*.

hardware   The physical components of a computer system.

Hayday, James (1796–1872)   A famous English bookbinder who introduced many improvements in binding practice. His method of sewing permitted books to open more easily.

head (1) The top of a page. (2) Word or phrase used to indicate the division of a book into chapters or other subdivisions. The style of type often indicates whether the division is a major or minor one.

head and tail pieces Ornamental designs printed at the beginning and end of a chapter or division of a book.

head margin The blank space above the first line on the page. *See* margins.

headband (1) A small band of silk or other material which is attached at the top or bottom (or both) of the spine of a book to add to its appearance. On finely bound books, the headbands are sometimes sewed in, stitch by stitch.

headline Display of type set above the text to which it refers. *See also* caption.

hellbox Box or receptacle in a printing office into which broken or discarded type is thrown.

Heures *See* Book of Hours.

hieroglyphics Characters (figures or objects) used in the picture writing of the ancient Egyptians, Thebans, Mexicans, etc.

high-speed printer Generally any type of computer printout device designed specifically for producing hard copy only, as opposed to an automatic typewriter which operates at much slower speeds and also has a keyboard for input purposes. Most high-speed printers have been of the chain printer type, but new machines now incorporate electrostatic and ink-jet printing principles. *See also* chain printer; electrostatics; ink-jet printing; line printer.

high-speed reader Any device that reads data into a computer at speeds compatible with the computer's internal processing speeds. Various types include tape readers and optical page readers. *See also* tape; optical character recognition.

hinges *See* guards.

Hoe, Robert (I, 1784–1833) Born in Leicestershire, England, emigrated to America in 1803. In 1805 he founded, in New York City, a firm for the construction of large printing presses. In the century following, the firm of Robert Hoe & Company did more for the improvement of machine printing than any other agency of their time. Hoe's son, **Richard March Hoe** (1812–1886) succeeded to the management of the firm of which his brother **Robert Hoe II** was also a member) in 1833. In 1847 Richard M. Hoe developed the "Hoe Type Revolving Machine," a great press which revolutionized newspaper printing. Upon his death in 1886, he was succeeded by his nephew **Robert Hoe III** (1839–1909), who himself devised various improvements in printing machinery and developed color presses.

Robert Hoe III was a great book collector and patron of the arts. He brought together the most famous and diversified private library of his time in America. Under the terms of his will the library was sold at auction in New York in 1911–1912. The sale created a tremendous stir, extending to Europe, and the bidding throughout was spirited. The most important event of the sale occurred on its first evening, April 14, 1911, when Hoe's copy of the Gutenberg Bible was acquired by George D. Smith (acting for Henry E. Huntington) for $50,000, the highest price ever paid up to that time for a printed book.

Hoe was active in everything that pertained to books. The Grolier Club of New York, the oldest existing American club devoted to the arts of the book, was founded at his house in 1884 by him and eight of his book-collector friends, and he served as the club's first president.

hollow-back   A book in which the back of the cover is not glued to the spine of the book, permitting it to bow outward when the book is opened.

hologram   A recording on photographic film of a three-dimensional image which can be reconstructed in three dimensions by passing coherent light through the film. *See also* holography.

holograph   A document wholly in the handwriting of the person from whom it proceeds. *See also* a.c.s.; a.d.s.; a.l.s.; etc.

holography   The process of making holographs by lensless photography which employs a laser light source.

Horae   *See* Book of Hours.

hornbook   A thin sheet of paper mounted on a paddle-shaped wooden board, having on it the alphabet and sometimes the Lord's Prayer. The printed material was protected by a sheet of transparent horn. Used in England for learning the elements of reading, from the middle of the fifteenth century and common down to the time of George II. Although the hornbook was used extensively in Colonial America in the seventeenth and eighteenth centuries, it is not known that any were locally produced. Genuine examples are now exceedingly rare. *See also* battledore.

Hornby, St. John   *See* Ashendene Press.

hot melt   A glue used in bookbinding which is applied hot and sets almost instantly when cooled.

hot metal   The processes of casting raised type from molten metal. The most common hot metal processes are linecasting (Linotype and Intertype),

Monotype and foundry casting. The latter two cast individual characters, while the former process produces a complete line of type at a time on a single piece of metal

Hours   *See* Book of Hours.

house style   Uniform manner of copy preparation followed by a particular publishing house with regard to grammar, spelling, punctuation, abbreviation, and other points of style.

Hroswitha   *See* book-collectors' clubs.

Hunter, Dard (1883–1966)   Leading authority on the craft of papermaking, on which subject he published many works. In 1939 he established the Paper Museum of the Massachusetts Institute of Technology.

hurt books   Damaged or shopworn books offered at sale prices.

hyphenation   In typesetting, the breaking of words at the ends of lines. A computerized typesetting system that does this automatically generally applies a set of hyphenation rules to the problem of determining proper breaking points. Because of the many exceptions to such rules in any language, however, such automatic hyphenation programs also usually rely on an exception dictionary of words which do not break according to the rules. Such words are broken according to special instructions for that word in the dictionary. Accuracy of such programs, equipped with exception dictionaries, typically reaches only 97–98 percent of all words broken because some words spelled exactly the same are broken differently, depending on the particular definition being used. *See also* exception dictionary; justification.

hyphenation routine   The set of rules and procedures followed by a computer in breaking words at the ends of lines in computerized typesetting.

hyphenless justification   Justification of type lines without using word breaks of any kind. All space left in the line is distributed between words or, in some instances, between individual characters as well.

ILAB   *See* International League of Antiquarian Booksellers.

ISBD(M)   *See* International Standard Bibliographic Description for Monographic Publications.

ISBD(S)   *See* International Standard Bibliographic Description for Serials.

ISBN   *See* International Standard Book Number.

ISR   *See* information storage and retrieval.

ISSN   *See* International Standard Serial Number.

-iana   *See* -ana.

ibidem (ibid.)   Latin word meaning "in the same place."

iconography   A detailed list and description of the pictorial or sculptured material connected with a person, place, or thing.

ideal copy   In bibliography, ". . . a book which is complete in all its leaves as it ultimately left the printer's shop in perfect condition and in the complete state that he considered to represent the final and most perfect state of the book."*

idem (id.)   Latin word meaning "the same" or "the same as mentioned above."

idiot tape   Encoded tape for input to a computer which contains only codes for type characters. Instruction codes for line justification and hyphenation as well as many typographic format codes are omitted, to be put in later by the computer.

illuminated   Embellished with ornamental letters, scrolls, miniatures, and other designs, usually in gold and color. A feature of many ancient manuscripts and early printed books.

illus.   Abbreviation for illustrations, or illustrated.

imperfect   A book lacking some leaves or whole signatures, or with leaves or sections either omitted, duplicated, misplaced, or damaged.

imperial octavo   *See* book sizes.

import   In the book industry, a book brought into a country upon or after its publication in another. The importer may act as one of several distributors, or may obtain sole distribution rights within a given area; he may in the latter case place his own imprint on the title page.

imposition   The operation of arranging pages for presswork so that when printed and folded the page numbers will be consecutive and the margins correct.

impression   The total number of copies printed at one time. *See also* edition.

imprimatur   Latin for "let it be printed." Official approval or license (secular or ecclesiastical) to print or publish a book. Such licenses, usually printed on the verso of the title page, and sometimes on a separate leaf, were common in the sixteenth and seventeenth centuries. The term is still used

---

*Bowers, Fredson T. *Principles of Bibliographical Description.* Russell and Russell, 1962. Reproduced by permission of the publisher.

today by the Roman Catholic Church which requires that any work—Bible, catechism, theological tract, liturgical book—that purports to represent authentic Catholic teaching have imprimatur. *See also* cum licentia; cum privilegio.

imprint (1) The name of a publisher, usually with the place and date of issue, generally placed at the bottom of the title page; occasionally, the name of the publisher's subsidiary or division under which a book is issued. (2) Name and address of a dealer on advertising material. (3) The name of a printer on any printed matter.

in press In process of production.

in print Obtainable from the publishers.

in quires The British term for *in sheets. See also* quire.

in sheets *See* sheets.

incunabula (*sing.* **incunabulum**) Latin word for "things in the cradle." The word is used to designate books printed from movable metal type before A.D. 1501, the last half of the fifteenth century being considered "the cradle of printing," during which period over 39,000 separate editions were printed. The Anglicized form *incunable* (pl. *incunables*) came into use in the nineteenth century. *See also* Gesamtkatalog der Wiegendrucke; Hain, Ludwig.

indention The setting of a line of type to a measure that is narrower than the full width of the type page or column. Quoted matter is often thus set. *See also* hanging indention.

index (*pl.* **indexes; indices**) An alphabetical list of names, places, and topics treated in a book, giving page numbers. Usually printed at the back of the book.

Index (1) *Index Librorum Prohibitorum*, the list of books that Roman Catholics were prohibited from reading as dangerous to their faith and morals; the latest list was issued in 1948; the publication was terminated in 1966. The list named only those books on which Church authority had been asked to rule. Some categories (not specific titles) remain prohibited under canon law. (2) *Index Expurgatorius,* a list of passages to be expunged or altered in works otherwise permitted; out of use today.

India paper An extremely thin but opaque paper used for thin-paper editions of books. *See also* Oxford India paper.

Indian Bible *See* Eliot, John.

inferior figures Small numerals, thus $_2$, used in formulas or to designate a specific leaf in a book.

information interchange format. *See* bibliographic information interchange format.

information processing All technical and commercial operations performed by computers. Normally used in a more general sense than the term data processing.

information storage and retrieval (ISR) The process of retrieving documents from a storage place in response to a person's query; this may be a manual operation (e.g., a librarian taking a book off of a shelf in the library) or a machine operation involving a computer, a data base, or other automated records.

initial letter A large capital or decorated letter used to begin a chapter section and sometimes a paragraph.

ink-jet printing A printing process in which tiny droplets of ink are squirted onto the paper through tiny nozzles. The nozzles can be turned on and off at computer speeds by means of digital signals as the paper passes in front of the nozzles. Characters thus can be formed by selective control of the ink jets. Ink-jet printing is used primarily in computer printout devices today, but experimental full-color prints of high graphic arts quality have been made, and the process may one day find a place in the regular printing industry.

inlaid binding A leather binding into which other colors or kinds of leather have been inserted for decorative purposes. Also known as mosaic binding. *See also* onlay.

input Data or instructions to be placed into a computer system. Input devices, used to input material into a computer, are of several types including keyboard units, optical character recognition units, tape readers, etc. *See also* keyboard; optical character recognition; high-speed reader; reader.

input-output (I/O) General term for devices for getting data into a computer and bringing it out. Often a single device can be used for both functions.

inserts Illustrations, maps, or other material not printed as part of the regular signatures, but in special sections instead. These are inserted in the book during binding. *See also* tipping in.

instruction A set of codes which defines something to be done by the computer with the data given it.

intaglio printing From the Italian "intagliare," to cut in. One of the four basic methods of printing, the others being relief, lithographic, and screen process printing. The printing areas on an intaglio printing plate are depressed so that when the entire plate is flooded with ink and then wiped, ink remains in these depressed areas in proportion to their depth. This is the opposite of relief printing where the ink is held by the raised surface, as on type or woodcuts. The intaglio method is the one used in etchings, steel and copper engravings, photogravure, and rotogravure.

interface   The point of contact between different parts of a system, different systems, or humans and the machine system.

interleaved   Any special leaves individually inserted between the printed leaves.

internal storage   Storage of data in a memory that is an integral part of the main computer, as opposed to a device which is auxiliary and can be detached.

International League of Antiquarian Booksellers   ILAB, or LILA (Ligue Internationale de la Librairie Ancienne), founded in 1948, is now made up of national associations of antiquarian booksellers of sixteen countries: Austria, Belgium, Brazil, Canada, Denmark, Finland, France, Germany, Great Britain, Italy, Japan, Netherlands, Norway, Sweden, Switzerland, and the United States. The League publishes an international directory of member-booksellers and an international glossary of book-collecting terms in eight languages. The current President of the League was elected at the 22nd Congress of the League (Tokyo, September 22–27, 1973): Dr. Frieder Kocher-Benzing, of the Stuttgarter Antiquariat, Rathenaustrasse 21, Stuttgart, Germany. *See also* Antiquarian Booksellers' Association of America, Inc.

International Standard Bibliographic Description for Monographic Publications [ISBD(M)]   A recommended international standard for the communication of bibliographical information for monographic publications. The ISBD(M) specifies the elements which should comprise a bibliographical description, the order in which these elements should be presented, and how they should be punctuated. Its objectives are: to make records from different sources interchangeable; to facilitate the interpretation of records across language barriers; and to facilitate the conversion of bibliographic records to machine-readable form.

International Standard Bibliographic Description for Serials [ISBD(S)]   A recommended international standard for the communication of bibliographical information for serials. The ISBD(S) specifies the requirements for the description and identification of serial publications, the order in which the elements of the description should be presented, and how they should be punctuated. Its objectives are: to make records from different sources interchangeable; to facilitate the interpretation of records across language barriers; and to facilitate the conversion of bibliographic records to machine-readable form.

International Standard Book Number (ISBN)   An international standard for exclusive identification of books. An International Standard Book Number identifies one title, or edition of a title, from one specific publisher, and is unique to that title or edition. A Standard Book Number was developed by British publishers in 1967, and adopted by the United States the following year. In 1969, the numbering system became an international standard known as the International Standard Book Number. The ISBN is usually printed on the verso of the title page, as well as in some prominent position on the outside of the book, as at the foot of the outside back cover or at the foot of the jacket if the book has one. On some paperback books, the ISBN is printed also on the lower part of the spine to facilitate inventory control. Most U.S. publishers are now participating in the program, which, when fully implemented, is expected to enable librarians, publishers, wholesalers, and booksellers to handle more effectively the writing, processing, and filling of orders. In the United States, the ISBN Agency is a collaboration between the Association of American Publishers, the American National Standards Institute—Committee Z 39, the Library of Congress, and the R. R. Bowker Company. There are similar agencies in other countries.

International Standard Serial Number (ISSN)   An internationally accepted code for the identification of serial publications. The ISSN program was developed by the International Organization for Standardization Technical Committee 46, and became operative in the United States in 1971 through the cooperative efforts of the Library of Congress, the American National Standards Institute, and the R. R. Bowker Company. All serials subscribed to by major libraries and currently being abstracted and indexed in the standard services are included in the program. The ISSN appears in a prominent place on each issue of a serial, usually the upper right corner of the front cover. When the program is fully implemented, the ISSN number can be used as a code by indexing and abstracting services, by subscription agents for communications, billing, inventory, claims, etc.; by authors for copyright; by publishers for inventory, ordering, and billing; and by library users for location of the item in the library. In library processing, the ISSN can be used for identification, control on acquisitions (check-in), claiming, accessioning, shelving, cooperative cataloging, etc.; in library reference for retrieval/request identification, interlibrary loan, etc. In machine use, the ISSN will fulfill the need for file update and linkage, retrieval and transmittal of data.

interpret   In computer processing, the translation of data in coding of one type into that of another type, or into human-readable form.

interrupt   To temporarily stop the normal computer routine, on special signal. Usually the normal routine can be resumed later.

Intertype   A line casting machine substantially the same as the Linotype.

introduction   A preliminary portion of a book leading up to the main subject matter. An *introduction* is usually an attempt to define the organization and limits of a work; a *preface*, by contrast, may explain the author's reasons for undertaking the work, his qualifications, his indebtedness to other authorities, etc. *See* front matter.

inventory   Total stock of materials for sale in the possession of a supplier or seller at a given time.

inverted entry   *See* catchword entry.

invoice   In book publishing, a publisher's bill showing precise, itemized quantities, prices, discounts and terms, and net amount due, for a shipment of books.

invoice symbols   The following symbols are often used on publishers' invoices:

C, OC—Order cancelled
EX—See explanation herewith
NE, NEP—New edition pending
NOP—Not our publication, cannot supply
OP—Out of print
OPP—Out of print at present
OS—Out of stock
NYP—Not yet published
TOP—Temporarily out of print
TOS—Temporarily out of stock
W—Will advise in a few days

issue   ". . . all the copies of that part of an edition which is identifiable as a consciously planned printed unit distinct from the basic form of the ideal copy. The criteria are that the book must differ in some typographical way from copies of the edition first put on the market, yet be composed largely of sheets deriving from the original setting; and that the copies forming another issue must be a purposeful publishing unit removed from the original issue either in form (separate issue) or in time (reissue)."* *See also* edition; impression; reissue; ideal copy.

*Gaskell, Philip. *A New Introduction to Bibliography.* © 1972 Oxford University Press. By permission of The Clarendon Press, Oxford.

italic Sloping types, as distinct from roman types, e.g., roman, *italic*. First used by Aldus Manutius in a Virgil which he printed in 1501. According to tradition, the style was closely copied from Petrarch's handwriting. A distinction is made between true italic characters, with their resemblance to handwriting, and "oblique" or "inclined roman" characters, which are uncommon but do exist. The most obvious difference is between the italic *a* and the inclined roman a.

In preparing copy for the printer, or in correcting proof, a single line under a word means set in *italics*.

Ives, Frederic E. (1856–1937) American inventor who developed the half-tone photoengraving process and made many contributions to the technique of color printing.

jacket *See* dust jacket.

jacket band A strip wrapped around a book jacket for sales promotion purposes; e.g., to emphasize some local or late news tie-in. *See also* dust jacket.

Jansen A style of hand bookbinding without line or ornament on the leather, either in gold or blind. There may be decoration on the inside of the cover, but absolute plainness on the outside, with the exception of lettering. The name is said to be derived from the Jansenists, an ascetic sect that flourished in the seventeenth century.

Japan paper An exceedingly strong high-grade paper made in Japan, used for printing etchings, photogravures, books, and also for binding; *French Japon* is a good imitation, less expensive and not so strong; American imitations are sometimes called *Japan vellum*.

Japanese style *See* Chinese style.

Jenson, Nicolas (1420?–1481) Celebrated printer of the fifteenth century. In 1458 he was sent by Charles VII of France to go to Mainz and discover the new art of printing. This he did, and returned to Paris in 1461, but owing to the death of Charles VII the project of setting up a press was abandoned.

In 1470 he established his own press at Venice. His Roman typefaces influenced printers down to modern times.

job lots Books offered by the publisher or wholesaler at special low prices to close out or cut down stock; *See also* remainders.

job press A small press, commonly of the platen type, upon which small letterpress jobs are done.

job printer   A printer who handles circulars, forms, stationery, book jackets, etc. He is a jack-of-all-trades compared to the printer who has specialized in books, magazines, labels, or some other line.

jobber   *See* wholesaler.

joint   The hinge joining the side of a book cover with the spine.

joint author   A person who writes a book in collaboration with one or more associates.

Julian Calendar   *See* calendar.

justification; justify   Lines of type are usually spaced out (either by distributing space evenly between words or by adding thin spaces between characters) to uniform width in order to have an even right-hand alignment. Type so handled is said to have right-hand justification. This paragraph is an example of right-hand justification.

In some instances, it is considered preferable, for aesthetic or for technical reasons, not to set type justified, or as a block, but give the right-hand edge an irregular appearance, usually known as ragged right. This paragraph is set ragged right to show the difference.

justification routine   The procedures a computer follows in calculating the required spacing to justify a line of type.

juveniles (n.); **juvenile** (adj.)   Children's books or pertaining to them. The terms, *children's books* and *junior books*, are increasingly preferred.

keep standing   An order to hold type, pending the possibility of reprinting.

keepsake   (1) One of the gift books, usually of verse and illustrated, in vogue in the early nineteenth century. (2) Printed mementos issued by clubs or organizations for special occasions. *See also* annuals.

Kells, Book of   Illuminated manuscript of the Latin Gospels, found in the ruins of the Abbey of Kells, Ireland, and thought to date from the eighth or early ninth century. It is now in Trinity College, Dublin.

Kelmscott Press (1891–1898)   A private press at Hammersmith, London, founded and directed by William Morris from 1891 to his death in 1896. The books issued from it were exceptional examples of bookmaking, and their beauty of execution and harmony of design were the result of exacting study. The paper and ink were especially made for the books, and three fonts of type were designed, the Golden, the Troye, and the Chaucer, the last used in a folio edition of Chaucer, one of the monuments of modern book printing.

kern   A part of a letter that projects over or under adjacent letters or past the edge of its own body, e.g., many lowercase italic *f*'s.

key plate   The plate of maximum detail in a set of color plates to which other plates in the same set are registered.

keyboard   (1) To type out data or instructions on a keyboard device, to encode them for entry into a computer. (2) Typewriter-like devices for encoding data for computer processing.

keypunch   A keyboard designed for punching punch cards.

kill   Directions to the printer to melt down or distribute composed type matter not wanted.

Kittredge, William A. (1891–1945)   Printer and designer at R. R. Donnelley's Lakeside Press, Chicago. Responsible for noteworthy books and important printing exhibits.

Knopf, Alfred A. (1892–   )   Pace-setting American publisher of cosmopolitan and exacting tastes who set unusually high standards of literary and typographic excellence. Graduated from Columbia College in 1912, he worked with Doubleday and with Mitchell Kennerly before starting a firm in his own name in 1915. He and his wife Blanche Wolf Knopf (1894–1966) developed and sustained a list of major literary works of European and Asian writers in translation, and many outstanding American authors. He fostered particularly the work of the typographer W. A. Dwiggins (*q.v.*) in giving a distinctive quality of design to Knopf ("Borzoi") books.

Koch, Rudolf (1876–1934)   German type designer. With Klingspor Foundry, Frankfurt from 1906. His types, which had international influence, include the Kabel sans serif.

kraft paper   Paper made from wood by the sulfate process. It has excellent strength and durability, but will not bleach so white as the sulfite and soda papers generally used for books. The best wrapping papers are made of brown, unbleached kraft. A binding paper with a kraft base has good folding endurance. Kraft also is used as lining material on the backbone of a book.

L.C.   Library of Congress.

lc   Lowercase (*q.v.*).

l.p.   Large-paper edition (*q.v.*).

l.s.   (*pl.* ls. s.) Letter signed. A letter of which the text is not in the handwriting of the signer.

label   Title of a book printed or stamped on other material and affixed to its spine or sides.

lacing in   Method common to hand binding by which cords are carried through holes in the boards of the cover, the ends cut off, hammered down smooth, and firmly glued. The covering material is then pasted over the cover.

laid paper   Paper which, when held up to the light, shows fine parallel lines (wire-marks) and crosslines (chain-marks). The marks are produced naturally by the wires of the mold in handmade papers and can be imitated by a pattern on the first roller in a paper-making machine.

lambskin   A lamb's leather with a smooth finish, similar to calfskin, but short fibered and less durable.

laminated   Layers of two or more substances glued or adhered together. Book covers and jackets often are laminated to an outer film of clear plastic to protect their printed surfaces.

Lane, Sir Allen (1902–1970)   Founder of Penguin Books in 1936, and head of the worldwide paperback publishing house until his death. Apprenticed at seventeen to John Lane at the Bodley Head, where he learned publishing. In 1936, he resigned to start his own firm. He became recognized as the modern pioneer in the successful paperback publishing of nonfiction, classics, and other serious books, along with quality fiction and children's literature. He was knighted in 1952.

language   A system for defining meanings and communicating them between people, or between people and machines. *See also* artificial language; machine language; natural language.

Lanston   *See* Monotype.

large-paper edition   A special edition printed from the same type as the standard edition, but with margins of extra size.

large post octavo; large post quarto   *See* book sizes.

lateral reversal   Change of an image from right to left or from left to right, producing a mirror image of the original. Metal type is laterally reversed from the print it makes on paper. Normal emulsion-to-emulsion contact printing with photographic materials produces laterally reversed images. Special reversal films, however, permit the copy to retain the original image direction.

law binding   A style of plain calf or sheepskin binding used for law books. Known also as *law calf* and *law sheep*. Buckram has largely replaced sheepskin, which, being a short-fibered skin, has a tendency to dry out and break at the hinges.

laydown speed   In phototypesetting, the speed at which characters are exposed on photographic material.

layout The working diagram of a page or other spatial area to be made up in type, for the printer to follow. Usually marked to show placement and spacing of text, headings, illustrations, captions, etc., with notes on the sizes and kinds of type to be used.

leaded matter Composition with space between the lines. In metallic composition, strips of material in the form of leads are inserted to create the spaces. Leads are two-point unless specified thicker. Most compositions systems today, both metallic and photographic, are equipped to space the lines as part of their setting function, thereby eliminating the need for a separate operation to add space between lines.

leaders (1) Dots or dashes set in succession so as to lead the eye, as in a table of contents. (2) The books of outstanding importance in a publisher's list of new publications.

leads Thin strips of metal, usually two points in thickness (1-36th of an inch) less than type-high, placed between successive lines of type, in order to increase the white space between them. Double leads call for two strips. Similar wooden strips are called *reglets*.

leaf A single sheet in a book containing two pages, one on each side.

leaflet A printed sheet folded but not stitched, sewn, or otherwise bound.

lean matter *See* fat matter.

leased line The rental of a telephone line or other communication channel for the exclusive use of the renter.

legend (1) On a map or chart, the key to various signs and symbols used. (2) The brief wording which identifies or explains an illustration. Present usage favors the word *caption* (*q.v.*) for this meaning.

lending library *See* rental library.

letter spacing The placing of spaces between the letters of a word. Letter spacing of text is not considered good practice by most typographers but in words or headlines composed exclusively of uppercase letters, letter spacing is often done.

letterpress The original Western invention of typographic printing, generally attributed to Johann Gutenberg of Mainz, Germany, about 1445. The dominant printing process for books until about the middle of the twentieth century when offset lithography became a serious competitor in book production. Letterpress is classified as relief printing because the printing areas, containing the typeface, are raised, or stand in relief, above the supporting, nonprinting structure, so that ink can be rolled on and then transferred by pressure to the paper.

lettre de forme; lettre de somme; lettre de batarde   The three general classifications of gothic type forms as found in the fifteenth century. The first is the Pointed and most formal; the second is the Round and less formal; the third is a Cursive form. They correspond to similar classifications of lettering used in the manuscripts that preceded printing.

level   Synonym for channel, usually used to describe the number of rows of code holes across a paper tape. *See also* channel.

Leypoldt, Frederick (1835–1884)   German immigrant who became an organizer of the American book trade. After operating his own bookstore in Philadelphia, he invited Henry Holt to join him in a publishing partnership in New York. The house organ of the firm was the *Literary Bulletin*, a compendium of general book news, and the precursor of numerous bibliographic tools. Leypoldt and Holt separated, Holt keeping the publishing enterprise, and Leypoldt the bibliographic program. In 1872 Leypoldt became the first editor of the *Publishers Weekly*; he originated the scheme of binding up publishers' catalogs, later to be known as the *Publishers Trade List Annual*; and he began or proposed other bibliographic tools that later became standard. Leypoldt, R. R. Bowker, and Melvil Dewey started the *Library Journal* in 1876, and helped found the American Library Association. In 1879 Leypoldt sold the *Publishers Weekly* to Richard Rogers Bowker (*q.v.*), his associate, who, with Mrs. Leypoldt, carried on the business after its founder's death.

libel   Any statement or representation which holds a person or corporation up to contempt and ridicule or pecuniary loss. Whether the statement be true or false, it is still libel, but damages can only be collected if false. It is up to the defendant to prove the truth of his allegation. Slander is verbal (spoken) libel.

library binding   *See* binding.

library edition   An edition, often of a children's book, in an especially strong binding for library use. *See also* binding.

Library Journal   Comprehensive professional journal of the American library world; founded 1876 by Frederick Leypoldt, R. R. Bowker, and Melvil Dewey (*q.q.v.*). Published by the R. R. Bowker Company.

Library of Congress catalog card   A printed catalog card issued by the Library of Congress for the use of libraries throughout the United States. As the L. C. Card Division catalogs books for its own collections, it prints extra cards which are available on a subscription basis, or which may be ordered by number. A publisher may request a card number from L. C.'s Cataloging in Publication office as soon as his book is in galley form, so that this number can be printed with the copyright information on the verso of the title page. Thus the librarian can order the catalog card by number upon receipt of the book. *See also* cataloging in publication.

Library of Congress classification   A system, often referred to as L. C., for classifying and shelving books, developed by the Library of Congress, for its collections.

The Library of Congress makes its catalog cards available to other libraries, showing on them both its own L. C. shelf numbers and the Dewey Decimal Classification numbers (*q.v.*), and also its determination of the places in its card catalog where such entry is to be duplicated.

ligature   Two or more letters cast as one piece, such as fi, ff fl, ffi, æ, ct, etc. *See also* logotype.

light pen   A light detection device shaped like a writing pen, attached to a video display terminal. When pointed to a particular spot on the display screen, the pen senses light and sends a signal to the computer which is used to tell where on the screen to perform operations. An alternative to the light pen is the use of a cursor on the screen. *See also* cursor.

lightface   A term used to distinguish ordinary type, as used in this sentence, from **boldface.**

limited edition   An edition of a volume or a set of volumes, of which a stated number of copies is printed. These copies (or sets) are usually numbered consecutively. A special page gives the facts as to the edition limit and the number, and often contains also the signature of the author, publisher, or printer.

Limited Editions Club   American subscription book club founded in 1929 by George Macy, and specializing in finely designed and printed works for its members. Through its policy of engaging the best designers and printers, here and abroad, the club has furthered the arts of the book, and brought them home to many who were not previously collectors, both through the parent organization and the Heritage Press, which has unlimited membership. The Club also has a controlling interest in the English Nonesuch Press.

limp binding   A binding from which the stiffening board has been omitted. *See also* flexible binding.

line cut; line engraving   A photoengraving on metal, usually zinc or copper, of a design in lines, dots or masses, without gradations of tone. The original design is transferred to the metal by photomechanics in such a way as to apply an acid-resist to the areas that are to take ink. The rest of the surface is eaten down by acid, leaving the design in relief. A *zinc etching* is a line cut on zinc. *See also* halftone.

line drawing   A drawing containing no grays or middle tones; for example, a pen-and-India-ink drawing, a scratchboard drawing, etc. In general, any drawing, including stippled or textured drawings, that can be reproduced without the use of halftone (*q.v.*) techniques.

line printer   A computer output device that prints one line of characters at a time across a page. *See also* high-speed printer.

linecasting machine   A hot metal typesetting device that casts a complete line of type on one bar of metal. *See also* hot metal.

linen   *See* book cloth.

linen paper   Originally any paper made from linen rags, but the term now is often applied to paper finished with a pattern simulating cloth.

liner   A piece of kraft paper glued to the backbone of a book, as opposed to super (*q.v.*) lining.

lines per minute   In typesetting, a basic statement of the speed or throughput of a system. Usually expressed in terms of newspaper lines, which are typically 10½ to 11½ picas wide and contain about thirty characters.

lining   The material which is pasted down on the back of a book after it has been rounded and glued off. It reinforces the glue and helps hold signatures together. The best bound books are lined with *super* (also called *crash*) and kraft paper called *liner*. In cheaper editions either crash or paper only is used. The word also is often used for *endpapers* (*q.v.*).

lining figures   *See* numerals, Arabic.

lining papers   *See* endpapers.

Linofilm   A phototypesetting machine developed by Linotype that produces characters on film instead of in metal. It is similar in its results to other photocomposition systems.

Linotype   A typesetting machine which sets matter in metal slugs or solid lines. Hence its name (and pronunciation), line-o'-type. Generally used for newspapers and periodical publications and quite extensively for books until the advent of photographic and electronic systems. Invented and developed in the United States between 1876 and 1886 by Ottmar Mergenthaler. *See also* Monotype; Intertype; Ludlow Typograph.

list   All the titles a publisher has available for sale. It includes his entire backlist and his new books of the season. A publisher's "spring list," on the other hand, is the list of titles he is bringing out during the spring season.

list price   The price to the retail consumer as set by the publisher; published price.

literary agent   One who acts for the author in finding a publisher for his manuscript and in handling subsidiary rights; also known as an *author's representative*; also one who acts for publishers in finding special types of material that they need. The agent is paid on a commission basis by the author.

lithography   Originally, the printing from smooth, porous limestone as invented by Alois Senefelder in Munich, about 1796. Also known generically as planographic printing, because both printing and non-printing areas are on the same plane of the image carrier. The image carrier is chemically treated to be ink-receptive and water-repellent in the printing areas and water-receptive and ink-repellent in the nonprinting areas. Thus, only the image takes up the ink, which is transferred to the paper. Consequently, each printing cycle requires inking as well as dampening or moistening with a solution consisting mainly of water.

Commercial lithography has become a most important industry. Now a variety of thin plates made of metals, plastics, and paper is available, and image transfer is generally indirect, from the plate to a soft blanket and from the blanket to the paper. Indirect printing is widely known as offset in contemporary printing parlance. Offset, or offset lithography, has become a most important method for book printing, superseding letterpress in many projects.

live matter   Composed matter, plates, or cuts which are held for future use.

Liveright, Horace B. (1888-1933)   American publisher who in his brief years in the business (1917–1930) brought flair, commercial daring, and new writers into the field, and trained brilliant young future publishers (Bennett Cerf, Richard Simon, Julian Messner, and others). In 1917 he formed a partnership with Albert Boni under the firm name of Boni & Liveright, and the firm immediately announced the publication of the first volumes of the Modern Library (later acquired by Cerf and Donald Klopfer). Liveright authors included Dreiser, O'Neill, Edgar Lee Masters, Faulkner, and others.

Livre d'Heures   *See* Book of Hours.

location A place in computer storage where data may be stored and retrieved from. *See also* address.

locking up In letterpress, making secure a form of type matter in the metal frame known as a chase, preparatory to putting it on the press.

logic system The set of discrete steps in a computer program followed by the machine to perform various data processing tasks.

logotype; logo (colloquial) A group of letters cast as a unit. In advertising the term is sometimes used to denote a particular form or style of trade name set in type or drawn. *See also* ligature.

long page A type page longer than has been specified.

loop (1) Synonym for cycle. (2) Repeated execution of a series of instructions until a terminal condition is met. *See also* closed-loop system; open-loop system.

loose in binding Description of a book, the sections or entire innards of which are badly loosened from the case to a more serious degree than *shaken* (*q.v.*).

loss leader Merchandise advertised and sold at a loss to attract customers into a store, sometimes to create the impression that the store's other prices are also low.

lowercase (lc) (1) The small letters of a type font as distinguished from the capitals, or uppercase. So called because in hand-set type they were usually kept in the lower section of two cases holding the type assortment. (2) In proofreading, directions to substitute small letters for capitals. *See also* case.

Ludlow Typograph A machine for setting display type. Brass matrices are set by hand in a special stick. The assembled mats are put over a slot in a steel table and molten metal is forced up from beneath, thus casting the whole line in a single slug.

m.f. Abbreviation for *machine finish* (*q.v.*).

McCain sewing, stitching *See* sewing.

machine coated *See* coated paper.

machine finish (m.f.) Paper which has been made smooth and somewhat glossy by passing through several rolls of the calendering machine. *See also* calendering.

machine language A language designed to be read by a machine without any translating steps, as opposed to an artificial language or symbolic language which requires interpretation of its terms into machine language in the computer before its instructions can be executed. *See also* artificial language; natural language; symbolic language.

machine-readable   Encoded in machine language and therefore readable by the machine. *See also* machine language.

machine translation   Automatic translation of one representation to another in the computer. Such translations may include, in addition to the interpretation of programming languages, the translation of natural languages from one to another, such as Russian to English. *See also* artificial language; machine language; natural language; symbolic language.

machining   A term used in England for *presswork* (*q.v.*).

macro code   A single instruction code given the computer to represent a complex condition. The computer replaces this macro code with a series of predetermined discrete codes required to produce the final condition. Macro codes are a form of shorthand for reducing the work of putting material into a computer.

made-up copy   An incomplete book whose lack of a leaf, or more, has been made good by the addition of the missing leaf or leaves from another imperfect copy or copies of the same edition. The making-up of a copy of a rare and costly book is not frowned upon, but the makeup must be proclaimed and not concealed.

A modern example of a great made-up copy is the *Pilgrim's Progress* [first edition of Part I], 1678, sold in the Frank J. Hogan sale in New York in April 1946, for $8,000. This volume was made-up after 1921 from two (possibly three) imperfect copies, and upon completion it became one of only eleven complete copies known. It is now in the Library of Congress.

magazine   The part of a composing machine such as the Linotype in which the brass matrices of the letters are stored.

magnetic storage   Storage of data by magnetizing or demagnetizing specified memory areas in a computer. Magnetic storage types include core, disk, drum, and tape devices. *See also* storage.

Mahieu, Thomas   *See* Maioli bindings.

main entry   In a card catalog or index, the entry under which full information is given, usually the author entry.

main frame   Synonym for central processing unit.

Maioli bindings   Styles of bookbindings by Parisian binders for the sixteenth century French book collector Tommaso Maiolus (the latinized form of Thomas Mahieu, or Matthieu), secretary to Catherine de Medici. Mahieu, long thought to be an Italian, was a famous collector of about the same time as Jean Grolier (*q.v.*), and many of the bindings in his library used the same form of legend as the Grolier bindings, being lettered on the front cover: THO MAIOLI ET AMICORUM. Most of the bindings were richly gilt with medallion and foliage designs, decorated with flowing interlace strapwork, and with ornaments in outline or azured.

majuscule   From the Latin "majuscula," somewhat greater. Large letters or capitals. In opposition to minuscule or small letters. Used especially in reference to early roman alphabets. In French "majuscule" is used as a synonym for uppercase.

make-ready   In its broadest meaning, all operations to get a job ready for presswork. In letterpress using type forms, the leveling and lining up of the form on the press, as well as the regulating of the printing pressure, so that the final printed product will pass the respective quality standards. The function of make-ready is essentially the same in all printing processes and methods, but the procedures differ considerably. Modern printing conditions require maximum utilization of the press equipment and make-ready should cause minimum press down time.

makeup   In letterpress printing, a general term for taking the type from the galleys, putting it into page form, inserting illustrative cuts, dividing the matter into page lengths, and adding running heads, titles of subdivisions, folios, footnotes, etc. Also, the steps of assembling the pages into forms.
   In photographic and other kinds of nonmetallic composition different techniques are needed, such as paste-up or stripping, for example. In highly advanced systems of computerized composition, makeup is a programmed function, often designated as computerized pagination.

manila   Durable yellowish paper or board. Paper made from manila hemp is called rope manila.

manufacturing   In book production, the complete process of composition, printing, and binding of a book.

manuscript (MS)   Literally, handwritten material. (1) A handwritten book, document or other work. (2) A written or typewritten work of an author, to be used as typesetter's copy.

Manutius, Aldus   *See* Aldus.

marbling; marbled edges   The process of decorating sheets of paper, cloth, or the edges of books with a variety of colors in an irregular pattern like the veins of marble.

MARC (MAchine Readable Cataloging)   A communications format for the transmission of machine-readable catalog data developed at the Library of

Congress and distributed to libraries and other subscribers in the form of magnetic tapes. The numerous applications of MARC include the production of acquisitions lists, catalog cards, book catalogs, bibliographies, and book labels.

marginal head, marginal note   *See* marginalia.

marginalia   Notes or headings written or printed on the margins of a page, including *marginal notes, marginal heads, side notes.* Usually set in narrow measure in type different from text of page. *Footnotes* are printed in the bottom margin of the page and *shoulder notes* at the top outer corner of the page.

margins   The area around the edges of a page outside the main body of the printed or written matter. The traditional ratio is: top margin 2; outside 3; bottom 4; inside 1½. The four margins are also called head margin, fore-edge margin, lower or bottom margin, and back margin. The inner space between two facing pages is called the *gutter* or *back margin.*

mark-sensing   A technique of recognizing special marks or notations on documents, as compared to optical character recognition which senses alphanumeric characters.

markup   The difference between the cost of a commodity, e.g., a book, to the dealer, and the price at which it is sold by him; usually expressed as a percentage. Literally, the markup is the percentage by which the cost is increased to reach the retail price. In common retail practice, however, markup is often used to mean the same as *discount (q.v.)* In the antiquarian field, markup is stated in dollars and cents, not as a percentage.

mass-market paperbacks   Low-priced paperbound books, with covers designed for sales appeal, distributed chiefly through magazine or magazine-style channels, to newsstands, variety and drugstores, supermarkets, and other mass outlets; also to many general bookstores, college stores, and department stores. *See also* quality or trade paperbacks.

Massee, May (1883–1966)   Children's book publisher and editor, who set standards of literary and artistic excellence that decisively influenced modern juvenile book publishing. Massee, who had been a children's librarian, became editor of junior books at Doubleday in 1923 and founded in 1933 the Viking Press children's book department, which she headed until 1960. A memorial collection of children's books, manuscripts and working materials, with a research and seminar program, was opened in her name in 1972 at Kansas State Teachers College.

masthead   A statement of the name, ownership, etc., of a publication. Usually found at the head of the editorial page of a newspaper. In a magazine, it is usually on the editorial or contents page. Sometimes called the *flag*.

mat   *See* matrix.

matrix (*pl.* matrices)   (1) A metal mold in which type or plates are cast. (2) A mold of a page of type from which stereotypes are made (often called a *mat*, sometimes a *mold*).

matter   Any type whether in process of being set, or standing. It may be *live* matter or *dead* matter, *open* matter (leaded) or *solid* matter (without leads). The old terms, *fat* and *lean* matter, are still used to indicate the proportion of open spaces or break lines. The *fat*, of course, gives the compositor far less work to do than the *lean*.

Matthieu, Thomas   *See* Maioli bindings.

Mazarin Bible   *See* Gutenberg.

Mearne, Samuel   English binder of the seventeenth century who became in 1660 royal binder to Charles II. He is noted for the so-called cottage style of ornamentation in which rectangles of parallel lines break outward at the corners and/or in the center, resembling the gables of a roof.

measure   The length of a full line of a page or column, expressed in picas (*q.v.*).

mechanical   Meticulously prepared layout for engraver or printer, showing exact placement of every element, and carrying actual or simulated type and artwork.

mechanical binding   *See* binding.

mechanical pulp   *See* groundwood pulp.

medium octavo; medium quarto   *See* book sizes.

Melcher, Frederic Gershom (1879–1963)   Book industry leader, co-founder, in 1919, of Children's Book Week (*q.v.*), founder and donor of the Newbery and Caldecott Awards for children's books (1922 and 1937, respectively) and, in 1943, the Carey-Thomas Award for excellence in publishing; editor and co-editor (with Mildred C. Smith) of *Publishers Weekly* for forty years. Trained at Lauriat's Bookstore, Boston, and Stewart's, Indianapolis, he joined *PW* in 1918. He was a fervent and influential supporter of effective book trade organization; of the development of children's book publishing, bookselling, and library service; of book-focused librarianship; of excellence in book design; of copyright reform; of freedom from censorship.

memory   In the computer field, synonym for storage.

Mergenthaler, Ottmar (1854–1899)   *See* Linotype.

merging   In computer processing, the combining of two or more terms into one file. Sometimes referred to as tape merging because tapes are often used as the storage medium.

Meynell, Sir Francis   *See* Nonesuch Press.

mezzotint   An engraving from a copper plate on which the entire surface is slightly roughened. The portions intended to show highlights or middle tones are scraped and burnished while the shadows are strengthened. Very beautiful velvety effects are thus obtained.

Microforms   A general term embracing both microfilm, with its variations, and also micro-opaque processes such as Microcard, Microprint, Microlex.

All microforms are techniques for greatly reducing the printed page in the interests of saving both space and copying costs. Re-enlargement for reading is normally done by a special projection machine.

Microfilm is usually handled in rolls, either 16mm or 35mm wide. However, it may also be "unitized," i.e., cut up and embedded for ease of handling in IBM cards or the like. Microfilms may be either negatives or positives; being transparencies, they may be enlarged by reflection rather than projections.

Microfiche refers to sheet microfilm. The size of the fiche has not been universally standardized, nor has the number of images, but the standard of approximately 4 × 6 inches adopted by the U.S. government is the most widely used.

Micro-opaques are reduced-size images made on white paper by either photographic or printing processes. They must be enlarged by reflection rather than projections.

Several devices are available which not only provide for enlarging microforms on a screen, but which also make permanent enlarged copies on paper of any desired image at the touch of a button.

Mimeograph   A duplicating machine operating on the stencil principle, and used for printing forms, letters, price lists, etc. "Mimeograph" is a trade name for the stencil duplicator made by the A. B. Dick Co. Stencils are usually prepared in the typewriter.

miniature books   Books in small format issued since the middle of the eighteenth century. The dimensions vary from less than an inch square to approximately 2 × 1¼ inches. These miniature editions are numerous and include the poets, the Bible, almanacs, gift tokens, etc.

miniatures   Originally, hand paintings used to decorate the text of manuscript books. Currently, in books either printed or manuscript, the miniatures may be either printed or hand painted.

mint A word used by some catalogers in the antiquarian booktrade to denote condition "as new."

minuscule From the Latin "minusculus," rather small. The small roman letters as distinguished from the capitals or majuscules. In French "minuscule" is still used as a synonym for lowercase.

misprint An error made by the typesetter, also called typographical error, or "typo"; in proofreading called printer's error, and often marked "PE" In the antiquarian trade, misprints are frequently used to establish priority of an edition, but John Carter in his *A B C for Book-Collectors* points out the hazards of any such assumption. "In the days of the hand-press, indeed, corrections were commonly made in the type after some sheets had already printed off; and misprints were often so corrected. Yet the sheets will have been gathered for folding and binding without regard for priority of printing, so that corrected and uncorrected sheets will be combined indiscriminately in the finished copies of the book as handed across the counter on publication day."

missal A book containing the service for the celebration of the mass throughout the year. Sometimes loosely used for any book of devotions.

miter In both composition and hand binding, to bring materials together at an angle without overlapping; to join lines or rules at angles.

mnemonic In the computer field, symbolic substitute or abbreviation for a numeric code. Used extensively in computer programming to provide more easily read alphabetic representations of the numerical codes required by the machine.

mode A particular manner or convention of use in which a computer system is operated.

modem A device that accepts signals from a sending device and modulates them for transmission over a telephone line or other communications channel, and then demodulates received signals back into a form a receiving device can accept.

modern The usual designation for the family of typefaces exemplified by Bodoni, as distinct from *old style* (*q.v.*).

This line is set in Bodoni.

module An integrated unit of a system which can be interchanged readily with other "building-block" units.

mold *See* matrix.

monitor To watch over and supervise the correct operation of a system.

monograph A treatise on one particular subject.

Monophoto A phototypesetting machine developed by the British Mono-type Corporation, distinguished by highest product quality but limited in its usefulness by very low speed. Only of historical interest in the United States.

Monotype A typesetting machine of American origin invented by Tolbert Lanston about 1888. Keyboard action causes holes to be punched in a roll of paper. The punched paper then controls a separate type caster. The lines of type which come from the caster are not solid slugs (like Linotype); each character is separate, like hand-set type. The Monotype is used for certain books, especially those containing technical signs, tabular matter, etc.

montage The combination of several pictures or parts of pictures blended into a single unit.

Morison, Stanley (1889–1967) English typographic adviser, designer and scholar, who gave strong impetus to typographic excellence in Western design. For forty years, from 1923, he inspired and guided the Monotype Corporation's program of reviving and modernizing fine classic typefaces; he maintained Cambridge University Press typography at an exemplary level; he modernized the look of the *Times* (London) and designed the new *Times Roman* typeface, and wrote numerous scholarly studies including *Type Faces and Type Design, English Liturgical Books, First Principles of Typography, The Typographic Book, 1439–1955*, and many more.

morocco A leather made from goatskin. Morocco is classed as one of the most durable leathers for bookbinding. It is very firm, yet flexible, and is usually finished on the grain side. Said to have been first made by the Moors.

 Levant morocco is a fine, heavy quality with a coarse grain. *Turkey* and *French* morocco are a finer grain, yet heavy in quality. *Niger* morocco is a fine goatskin with a natural finish. Tanned on the banks of the Niger River, it is an acid-free leather used for expensive bindings. *Persian* morocco, having a still finer grain, is made from Persian goatskins. Many imitations are made from sheepskin.

 The history of binding begins with the introduction of this leather and gold tooling at the end of the fifteenth century in Venice and Florence. The goatskins came from the Levant, where they had long been in use. Gold tooling is said to have been used in Syria at least as early as the thirteenth century, and both this and morocco were first made familiar in Europe through the Italian trade with the East. The earliest European bindings in morocco with gilt decoration so commonly occur upon books printed by Aldus, the great Venetian printer, that many of them are supposed to have been made for him or under his supervision, and the Venetian covers of his time are usually called Aldine bindings.

Morris, William (1834–1896)   English poet, artist, author, and craftsman. Founder of the Kelmscott Press (*q.v.*) In 1888, Morris and a few friends undertook a revival of printing and bookmaking, which had its inspiration in a thorough knowledge of the art of the fifteenth century. No similar movement in modern times has had such a powerful and far-reaching effect. Many fine presses were established as a result of his pioneering.

mosaic binding   *See* inlaid binding.

Mosher, Thomas Bird (1852–1923) Former sea captain turned publisher and book designer in Portland, Maine. From 1891 he produced a long list of belles lettres, many of them pirated, in formats of delicacy and taste. From 1895 through 1914 he published, in monthly form, *The Bibelot, A Reprint of Poetry and Prose for Book Lovers,* chosen in part from scarce editions and sources not generally known. This publication was later reissued, bound in twenty volumes, and an index volume to the whole was added.

mottled calf   An ornamental treatment of calf, producing, by ink or acid, a variegated pattern; called *tree calf* when the pattern resembles the grain of gnarled wood.

movable type   The apparatus for casting movable type was developed by Gutenberg (*q.v.*) in the middle of the fifteenth century. The actual invention of printing with movable type was probably not made by any one man. There are stories about Coster of Haarlem, there are legal documents relating to Gutenberg at Strasbourg and Mainz as early as 1436 as well as notarial records of experiments by Waldfoghel at Avignon in 1444. But there are in existence no books or pieces of printing that can be definitely proved to have been printed by any of these three men.

   The important fact is that printing first became a business at Mainz, after 1445, and spread from there over the world. The first dated piece of type printing is an indulgence of Pope Nicholas V, of 1454.

   According to Thomas Francis Carter, a Chinese named Pi Shêng made movable type in the period Ch'ing-li (1041–1049), some 400 years before Gutenberg.

Moxon, Joseph (1627–1691)   London machine maker, printer, and type founder. Published the first of his "Mechanick Exercises" in 1677, the earliest printers' manual in English.

MS (*pl.* **MSS**)   Manuscript.

MS s. (*pl.* **MSS s.**)   Manuscript, signed. A manuscript of which the text is not in the handwriting of the signer.

Multilith   A small, in-plant offset press used for duplicating forms, form letters, etc.

multiple-access The principle of providing many access lines into a computer for use by more than one person at the same time. *See also* time-sharing.

multiprogramming A technique of running two or more programs in a computer at the same time.

Munsell, Joel (1808–1880) Printer, scholar, publisher, and bookseller in Albany; a successful commercial printer who was noted as well for his fine printing and book design. In 1856 Munsell printed his *Papers Relating to the Island of Nantucket*, the first book in America to make use of Caslon type. His *Chronology of the Origin and Progress of Paper and Papermaking* went through many editions.

NACS National Association of College Stores.

n.d. No date. In cataloging it indicates that no publication date is printed in the book described. If the date of publication is known but is not in the book the date is expressed thus: (n.d., 1850). If the date is in the book but not on the title page it is expressed thus: [1850].

NE, NEP Invoice symbols meaning "new edition pending."

NOP Invoice symbol meaning "not our publication, cannot supply."

n.p. No place of publication or no publisher given.

n.y. No year given.

NYP Invoice symbol meaning "not yet published."

narrow (nar.) *See* book sizes.

narrow-band Communication channels which can transmit data at slow speeds, up to 200 bits per second. *See also* broad-band; data transmission.

national bibliography Commonly, a list of books, current or retrospective, including the complete or near-complete publishing output of any one country.

National Book Awards Awards honoring literary excellence, presented annually since 1950 to authors of books in a variety of categories. Prize money was donated by various book industry organizations, and the awards had been administered by the National Book Committee (*q.v.*).

National Book Committee A nonprofit society founded in New York in 1954 and discontinued in 1974, devoted to the "wider and wiser use of books." The Committee supported the freedom to read, encouraged the wider availability of books, and sponsored National Library Week, the National Book Awards, the National Medal for Literature, and studies related to books and reading. The

Committee cooperated particularly with the American Library Association and the Association of American Publishers, among other national groups.

National Library Week A week-long annual promotional effort, and center of a year-round program for support of libraries, launched in 1958 and sponsored originally by the National Book Committee in cooperation with the American Library Association. When the National Book Committee discontinued operations in 1974, the program was taken over solely by the American Library Association. Specific purposes of the program are to encourage legislation favorable to libraries, expand library use to increasing numbers of people, and defend the freedom to read.

natural language A language whose rules permit changes in meaning and usage, as opposed to an artificial language which rigidly prescribes every definition prior to use. *See also* artificial language; machine language.

negative Usually a transparent photographic film on which both the light values and image are reversed—the black of the original subject is white, the light grey is dark grey, left is right, etc. A photostatic negative reverses black for white but, by using a mirror in the process, produces readable rather than mirrored lettering. A negative is the first step in printing by offset and it is usual, after printing, to hold the negatives (or perhaps positives made from the negatives) rather than the plates. A *positive* is the print made from a negative, with light values and image as in the original subject.

net Not subject to discount or reduction. The use of the term in connection with the retail price of new books in the United States began about 1900 when the publishers endeavored to end the then prevalent retail practice of cutting list prices.

The term "net" may also be applied to book prices carrying no discount to retailers, or to indicate that a wholesale price is subject to no *further* discount. For example an invoice may read "2% 10 days, net E.O.M." meaning that a further 2% "cash" discount will be allowed for payment within 10 days, after which the full "net" total is due by "end of month."

In 1899 the English publishers signed an agreement for the prevention of price cutting, called "The Net Book Agreement." When an English book carries no trade discount, it is sometimes called a "net net" book.

new (revised) edition An edition containing substantial revisions by the author or editor; *not* merely a new impression, a reprint, or a reissue from original plates which may or may not contain certain minor variations or corrections in format or text. *See also* edition.

nihil obstat Latin for "nothing hinders"; used by a Roman Catholic *censor* to attest that a book contains nothing damaging to faith or morals. *See also* imprimatur.

noise random variations in the characteristics of an element which tend to disturb or interfere with the normal operation of a device or system. Random fluctuations in electrical voltage or current, for example, tend to upset the operation of computer circuits.

nom de plume A pen name; a pseudonym; a writer's assumed name.

non-impact printer A class of printout units which create characters on paper without the use of typing principles. Photographic, electrostatic, or ink-jet techniques usually are used to create images.

nonbook materials Materials which do not meet the definition of a book or periodical (*q.v.*), such as audiovisual and vertical file materials.

Nonesuch Press Founded in London in 1923 by Francis Meynell, Vera Meynell, and David Garnett as publishers of fine editions of scholarly character. An interest in the Press was acquired in 1936 by the Limited Editions Club of New York.

nonpareil The old name for a type size half the size of pica. When a printer inserts a nonpareil of space, he inserts six points of space.

nonwoven materials Covering materials other than cloth used in bookbinding. Numerous types are made today including paper and various kinds of plastics. Paper and some plastics are composed of fibers matted into thin sheets, while other types of plastic materials are solid sheets of extruded or otherwise molded material. Many nonwovens combine different papers and plastics in one material, usually by lamination.

numerals, Arabic 1, 2, 3, 4, etc. The numbers from 0 to 9 began to appear in European manuscripts in the twelfth century, and their forms, especially the 4, 5, and 7, passed through various stages before reaching approximately the present forms. The Arabs, who gave this system to Europe, probably brought it from India in the eighth century. A legend attributes its introduction into Europe to Pope Sylvester II (999–1003).

Old style Arabic numerals as 1, 2, 3, 4, 5, 6, 7, 8, 9, 0, have ascenders and descenders. The exigencies of tabular work made it desirable to provide alternate "lining figures," thus, 1, 2, 3, 4, 5, 6, 7, 8, 9, 0.

numerals, Roman Numerals in the Roman system of notation are still used in the dating of certain books published today; in early bookmaking it was the general custom.

In the Roman system the following are the symbols chiefly used: $I = 1$; $V = 5$; $X = 10$; $L = 50$; $C = 100$; $D = 500$; $M = 1,000$.

Several rules govern the combinations used to express intermediate and higher numbers: (1) Any symbol *following* one of equal or greater value, *adds* its value. Thus $II = 2$; $VI = 6$; $LI = 51$. (2) Any symbol *preceding* one of greater value, *subtracts* its value. Thus IV = 4; XL = 40; CM = 900. (3) When a symbol stands *between* two of greater value, its value is subtracted from the second symbol and the remainder is added to the first. Thus XIV = 14; LIX = 59; MCM = 1,900. The shorter form achieved by subtraction is favored in modern usage: IX rather than VIIII for 9; MCM rather than MDCCCC for 1,900. "Thousands" are sometimes indicated by drawing a line over a numeral: as, $\overline{V}$ = 5,000; $\overline{C}$ = 100,000.

OC Invoice symbol meaning "order canceled."

OCR Abbreviation for optical character recognition.

o.k. with corrections A message to the printer that the proof is all right when indicated changes are made.

o.p. Abbreviation for "out of print" (*q.v.*).

o.p.c. Abbreviation for "out of print, canceled."

OPP Invoice symbol meaning "out of print at present."

o.p.s. Abbreviation for "out of print, searching."

o.s. Invoice symbol meaning "out of stock."

o.s.c. Abbreviation for "out of stock, canceled."

o.s.f. Abbreviation for "out of stock, to follow."

o.s.i. Abbreviation for "out of stock, indefinite."

o.s.t. Abbreviation for "out of stock, temporary."

oblique *See* italic.

oblong (obl.) *See* book sizes.

occult A classification for books relating to mysticism, clairvoyance, magic, theosophy, and related phenomena.

octavo (8vo) *See* book sizes.

odd sorts Characters not included in a font of type or composition system. Also known as *special characters*. Most systems have provisions for adding special characters. On a Linotype machine, for example, matrices from which odd sort characters are cast can be inserted by hand in lines where required. The need for special characters is an important consideration in selection of a composition system.

off its feet Metallic type is said to be off its feet when it does not stand square upon its base, thus creating an unequal impression.

off-line   Part of a computer system not connected directly by wire to the rest of the system. Materials must be hand-carried between the off-line part and the main computer. *See also* on-line.

offprint   A separate printing or reprint of an article or chapter which has appeared first in a magazine or some other larger work.

offset   In lithographic printing, a specific press design which transfers the ink twice between printing plate and the final sheet of paper to be printed. The image is first transferred from the plate to an intermediate rubberized blanket, and from this it is "offset" onto the paper. Virtually all lithography except certain special art prints today is produced on offset-type presses, and the term offset has become almost synonymous with lithographic printing. Many types of offset presses are used today, including web and sheet-fed equipment as well as single and multicolor presses. The use of the intermediate rubberized blanket permits printing of very fine detail such as fine-screen halftones on papers with rough or uneven surfaces.

offset paper   Paper that has been treated to give good results in offset printing.

Old English   An angular type of the black letter group, abbreviated O.E.

𝔒𝔥𝔦𝔰 𝔩𝔦𝔫𝔢 𝔦𝔰 𝔰𝔢𝔱 𝔦𝔫 𝔒𝔩𝔡 𝔈𝔫𝔤𝔩𝔦𝔰𝔥.

old style   Adaptations of the types of early printers, such as Garamond, Elzevir, Caslon. *See also* modern.

This line is set in Garamond.

omnibus book   (1) A reprint edition of several works of an author, complete or a selection, in a single volume. (2) A collection of a number of books or stories on a single subject by various authors in one volume.

on approval   May be returned if not wanted. Usually applied to a transaction allowing the customer the privilege of examining goods before purchase.

on consignment; on sale   Supplied on an agreement that copies need not be paid for until sold. *See also* returns.

on-demand book   A book manufactured as a single copy at the time a customer wants to buy it. On-demand systems are still not common, being used primarily to produce copies of scholarly works from master files of microfilms. The concept would eliminate major inventory problems but new technology is required before on-demand book manufacturing can become a large factor in the book industry.

on-line Part of a computer system connected to the rest of the system electrically via wires, so that data may be passed back and forth without delays or human handling. *See also* off-line.

on press *See* in press.

one shot (1) The reprinting in one issue of a periodical the full text or an abridgment of a book, as opposed to a serialized reprint. (2) A magazine of which there is but one issue. (3) A type of hot melt adhesive requiring only one application to bind a book.

onlay A leather binding onto which other colors or kinds of leather have been applied by pressure for decorative purposes.

ooze leather Calf or sheepskin with a suede-like finish. Usually split sheepskin finished on the flesh side.

opacity In printing papers, that measurable property which prevents the showing through of printed images, both pictures and text. Especially important in thin papers.

open-loop system System in which a series of automatic machine operations is interrupted by one or more human operations before the entire cycle is completed. *See also* loop; closed-loop system.

open-to-buy The amount of money available to the manager of a retail department (as in a department store) for new purchases in a given period, such as a month. Some book merchandisers consider this a controversial practice, sharply limiting the flexibility of book department operation.

operation A defined action which a computer will perform on instructions from its program.

optical center Somewhat above the actual center of a page. When material is thus centered on a page, it is not mathematically but optically centered.

optical character recognition (ocr) An optical-electronic means of reading printed or written data into a computer, converting it into machine-readable code in the process. When printed, typed, or even some kinds of handwritten characters are passed in front of an electric-eye scanning device, it senses light and dark patterns forming the characters. These sensings are converted to electrical impulses representing digital codes, and the computer then translates these codes into machine-language codes. In computerized typesetting, optical character recognition is used primarily to enter data into a computer. However, some editing functions can be performed with certain types of equipment if instructions for making changes are typed out for the scanner in the proper format. *See also* editing.

option The privilege to buy or sell a specific property, as a manuscript or rights to a book, usually within a given length of time.

original Finished camera-ready copy, suitable for reproduction. *See also* camera-ready.

original cloth; original boards; original wrappers In catalog description, the covers in which the book was first published.

original parts A catalog description of a work first issued in installments at regular intervals, monthly or weekly, in printed and illustrated wrappers. The most popular of these publications in the nineteenth century were the novels of Ainsworth, Dickens, Lever, Surtees, Thackeray, and Trollope.

ornament Any decorative device, such as a rule, border, initial letter, or design.

out of print (o.p.) The publisher's stock exhausted.

out of stock (o.s.) The publisher's stock temporarily exhausted.

output The results of computer processing which are brought out of the system in some form of display, printout, or storable memory device.

overlay (1) In letterpress presswork, the thin sheets of tissue placed under the tympan during the make-ready process to increase or equalize the squeeze or impression on the paper being printed. (2) In art work, the protective covering of paper, tissue, cellophane, etc. over the original material.

overprint (1) To revise printed matter by superimposing new information, sometimes blocking out unwanted images. (2) To print more than ordered. (*See also* overrun.) (3) In multicolor printing, to obtain different colors by printing various color inks over each other.

overrun Additional copies above the number ordered to be printed.

oversewn A method of binding or rebinding a book for extra strength, as for library use, in which each leaf is sewn individually into the book. Oversewing does, however, prevent the book from opening quite flat.

Oxford India paper Very thin, soft, tough, and opaque paper, used by the Oxford University Press and made at their Wolvercote Mill.

Ozalid A type of *blueprint* (*q.v.*).

p. (*pl.* **pp.**) Abbreviation for page.

PE (printer's error) *See* misprint.

p.p.   Abbreviation for "postpaid."

PPA   Publishers Publicity Associaton.

PTLA   Abbreviation for "Publishers Trade List Annual."

PW   Abbreviation for the *Publishers Weekly* (*q.v.*).

Pablos, Juan   First printer in the New World, an Italian who in 1539 produced in Mexico City a "Breve y Mas Compendiosa Doctrina Christiana" in Spanish and Mexican.

package   An integrated group of components in a computer system, such as a group of programs which operate together or a complementary set of equipment and programs.

Padeloup, Antoine Michel (1685–1758)   One of the most famous binders in France in the eighteenth century. Two generations of his family before, and two after him were prominent binders. He developed the *dentelle* or lace pattern in decoration, a style that succeeded the *pointillé* of Gascon.

page   One side of a leaf.

page break   The point in the text of a book where one page ends and the next one begins.

page map   A diagrammatic representation of a page layout on the screen of a cathode-ray tube. Depending on the sophistication of the computer program producing it, a page map is approximately equivalent to an artist's pencil-sketch layout of a page. In computerized page makeup, it is used to position typographic elements on a page area so that the computer can then specify for the typesetting machine where each element should be placed during typesetting. *See also* idea layout terminal.

page proofs   *See* proofs.

pagination   The numbering of the pages of a book. In electronic composition systems, pagination includes most or all functions of page makeup.

painted edges   *See* fore-edge painting.

paleography   (1) An ancient manner of writing; ancient writings, collectively. (2) The study of ancient inscriptions and modes of writing; the art or science of deciphering ancient writings.

palimpsest   Derived from Greek roots meaning, to rub away again. A parchment or other material from which the original writing has been more or less completely erased and new matter written over. A double palimpsest is one that has had two such erasures. Valuable texts have been recovered from such parchments.

pamphlet In the UNESCO definition, a complete unbound, nonperiodical publication of not fewer than five nor more than forty-eight pages exclusive of covers. In informal usage, a pamphlet is also considered, ordinarily, to be saddle-bound, with covers of the same paper as the text or of a heavier paper, and may run to many more than forty-eight pages. *See also* book.

pamphlet binding *See* binding; stitching.

Pannartz, Arnold *See* Sweynheym.

paper The sheets of matted cellulose fibers produced either by a handdipping process or on a Fourdrinier machine. Wood fibers are the main ingredient used in paper, although higher grades of writing papers are made with cotton fibers.

Book papers fall into several classes—those made from chemically prepared wood pulp as used in the general run of higher-priced books, and those made from acid-free ingredients. Paper may also be *coated* or uncoated, *sized* (for offset printing or to take pen-and-ink) or unsized, handmade (the only kind that is without *grain*, i.e., that does not bend or tear more easily in one direction than the other) or machine-made, *laid* or *wove*, etc. It also comes in a variety of surface finishes from rough to smooth and dull to glossy. *See also* basis weight; Bible paper; bulk; calendering; chemical pulp; coated paper; cockle; Fourdrinier; free sheet; grain; groundwood pulp; handmade paper; laid paper; linen paper; paper permanence; pulp; ream; wove paper.

paper-covered boards *See* boards.

paper covers A book covered with a printed or unprinted paper wrapper affixed to the book. Used generally in describing a book not bound in boards, cloth, or leather, such as a paperback or paperbound book. *See also* paperbound; wrappers.

paperback *See* paperbound.

paperbound A paper-covered book. More often called *paperback*. *See also* mass-market paperback; quality or trade paperbacks.

Paperbound Books in Print Index of paperbound books published and currently available in the United States. Issued several times each year by the R. R. Bowker Company.

paperbounder A publisher of paperbound books; a term popularized in the industry by Ian Ballantine.

paper permanence   The degree of resistance to deterioration that paper can be expected to possess. The single most important factor affecting the rate of paper deterioration is acid content. Other less important factors are heat, humidity, and atmospheric pollution. A high acid content will increase the tendency of paper to discolor and become brittle. The research of W. J. Barrow has shown that even one hundred percent rag content paper will deteriorate rapidly if the acid solutions used in its manufacture have not been neutralized. The reason that Gutenberg's paper has lasted five centuries while the best papers (including one hundred percent rag papers) of the early twentieth century have already become brittle has now been determined to be related to acid content.

Although a substantial quantity of paper used in today's printing (especially for newspapers and mass-market paperbacks) has a high acid content and thus a short life expectancy, many paper companies now market acid-free book papers, often called permanent-durable papers, which have a guaranteed life of several hundred years.

Libraries have become increasingly concerned with the physical condition of their collections, especially of books printed after 1800. These books are considered to be in imminent danger of deterioration, due mainly to the destructive materials used in paper production during the nineteenth century. Some of these harmful materials included alum for sizing, chlorine bleach for whitening, and calcium sulfate and barium sulfate for paper loading.

paper weight   *See* basis weight.

papyrus   (1) A form of paper used by the ancient Egyptians, made from the inner bark of a reed of the same name growing on the banks of the Nile. Prepared by laying strips over one another at right angles. Two or three layers were soaked in water and pressed into one sheet. The sheets were joined to produce a roll. (2) A manuscript written on this material.

parameter   A specific type of variable in a system which must be defined by someone for the system.

paraph   A flourish at the end of an autograph signature. In the Middle Ages this was a sort of rude safeguard against forgery.

parchment   A writing material, also used for bookbinding, made from the inner side of the *split* skin of a sheep, and prepared somewhat like vellum (*q.v.*). It was probably used as early as 1500 B.C. In the second century B.C., Eumenes, King of Pergamum, in Asia Minor, could not obtain sufficient papyrus from Egypt for his large library, so he had his entire library prepared on parchment made from the skins of sheep, goats, and pigs. This parchment became known as *Charta Pergamena*.

parity check   A means of testing the accuracy of data in a computer system through an automatic comparison process. Used extensively to check for errors made in recording or transmitting data.

part title   Same as divisional title (*q.v.*).

partial remaindering   Selling off at sale or "remainder" prices a portion of a publisher's unsold stock of a book, rather than the entire stock. Thus, some part of the stock remains in print to be sold at the publisher's list price, and both publisher and author gain by the sale of excess quantities. *See also* remainders.

paste-downs   *See* endpapers.

paste-up   (1) Assembly of opaque photographic paper or reproduction proofs containing type and other images into made-up sections or pages by means of pasting them down on a carrier sheet. The result is camera-ready copy (*q.v.*). (2) Assembly of proofs on a layout for guidance of the printer. *See also* dummy.

pasteboard   A stiff material made by pasting several sheets of paper one upon the other; any kind of paper board made by the union of thin layers of paper pulp.

pasting in   *See* tipping in.

patent base   A device for raising the level of the bed of a letterpress printing press so that electrotypes or stereotypes need not be mounted on wood.

pattern recognition   Identification of shapes, forms, or configurations by automatic means. *See also* optical character recognition.

Payne, Roger (1739–1797)   English bookbinder. He was a great craftsman, who is credited with inventing a method of wetting and rolling morocco leather to produce a "straight grain"; he is also regarded as the creator of a new style of binding decoration. The backs of his books were richly gilt, but the outer sides usually had only corner decorations, his elaborate gilt decorations being reserved for the doublures of his extra special bindings. His favorite designs consisted of crescents, circles, stars, running vines, etc., studded with gold dots. He designed his own tools for his gilt decorative finishing. He bound many of his books in Russia leather scented with birch oil; his morocco leathers were mainly of very deep colors of red, blue, olive, and orange. The bills he submitted for his work were as carefully prepared and set forth as his bindings; all the details, even the minutest, are listed, together with all the materials used, and a price is given for each step.

Penrose Annual   Review of the graphic arts, published in London since 1895.

perfect binding *See* adhesive binding.

perfecting press A press which prints both sides of a sheet before it leaves the press.

perforated tape Paper tape on which data has been encoded by punching rows of holes across the tape.

perforating The cutting of a line of tiny holes or slits in a sheet of paper to facilitate folding or later tearing of the sheet along the line. Done on either a regular printing press, a special cutting and creasing press or a folding machine by impressing a raised serrated rule or disk into the paper.

periodical "A serial appearing or intended to appear indefinitely at regular or stated intervals, generally more frequently than annually, each issue of which normally contains separate articles, stories, or other writings. Newspapers disseminating general news, and the proceedings, papers, or other publications of corporate bodies primarily related to their meetings, are not included in this term."*

peripheral equipment Auxiliary devices that may be attached to a computer system to enlarge the machine's basic capacity or to perform special functions.

Perkins, Maxwell Evarts (1884–1947) Editor whose guidance of numerous important American writers contributed substantially to their development. He joined Charles Scribner's Sons in 1910, was its chief editor, 1927–1947, and a company officer. His correspondence with Thomas Wolfe, Ernest Hemingway, F. Scott Fitzgerald, and many others provides fascinating insights into the conduct of author-publisher relations, as shown in *Editor to Author: The Letters of Maxwell E. Perkins*, edited by John Hall Wheelock, and *Dear Scott, Dear Max*, edited by John Kuehl and Jackson Bryer (both Scribners).

permanent-durable papers *See* paper permanence.

permission Clearance from a copyright owner to quote passages or reproduce illustrations from his property.

pH A chemical term denoting the acidity or alkalinity of a solution. In offset printing pH is a critical measurement for the water, or fountain solution, used in the process.

---

*This material is reproduced with permission from American National Standard Abbreviation of Titles of Periodicals Z39.5, copyright 1969 by the American National Standards Institute, copies of which may be purchased from the American National Standards Institute at 1430 Broadway, New York, N.Y. 10018.

photo offset lithography   *See* offset.

photocomposer   A precision machine used in offset platemaking where multiples of the same images must be exactly positioned and exposed. (Not to be confused with photographic typesetting equipment.)

photocomposition   (1) The process and product of photographic typesetting. (2) The making of multiple exposures of the same or varying subjects on a single photographic negative.

photoengraving   *See* engraving.

photogelatin   A printing process (also called collotype) often used for frontispieces, facsimile reproductions, and fine illustration work in general. Unlike the more common printing processes, photogelatin uses no screen. Delicate tones and fine details are reproduced without being broken up into halftone dots.

photographic typesetting   Used generally as a synonym for photocomposition, except that photocomposition can encompass film stripping or paper paste-up procedures for makeup operations, while photographic typesetting is limited to actual setting of type. *See also* photocomposition.

photogravure   *See* gravure.

photolettering   Use of a wide variety of devices for hand-positioning images to be set photographically on film or paper. Generally used for display and special typefaces. *See also* photographic typesetting; phototypography.

photolisting   Synonym for sequential card system.

photomechanics   Devices or manual operations which employ both photographic and mechanical principles.

photomontage   *See* montage.

Photon   Name of a corporation manufacturing photographic composition systems and equipment; also used for individual machines, often followed by a distinctive number.

Photostat   A device for making photographic copies of documents, drawings, printed pages, etc. The resulting image, which is "right-reading" and not mirror-wise, may be made the same size as the original, or enlarged or reduced. The first Photostat copy is a negative, reproducing white for black. If black for black is desired, a positive Photostat is made from the negative Photostat. The name Photostat is applied both to the machine and the resulting copies.

phototypesetting   Synonym for photographic typesetting.

phototypography Synonym for photocomposition, but with emphasis on typographic considerations.

pi character A miscellaneous character not part of a standard complement on a typesetting machine, but nevertheless required to produce certain types of work. The term pi comes from the printer's word for spilled or unsorted type.

pica (1) The printer's standard of measurement for length of lines and depth of type pages. A pica is equal to twelve points, or approximately one-sixth inch. (2) The old name for a type size measuring about six lines to the inch, equivalent to twelve point. (3) The larger of the two most used kinds of typewriter type having ten characters per inch and six lines per inch. (The other kind, *elite*, also has six lines per inch, but has twelve characters per inch.)

Pickering, William (1796–1854) English publisher and bookseller whose fine taste in book production made his imprint famous. He set up his own bookshop in 1820, and began publishing in 1821. Among his first publications were the early volumes of a series that became famous: the *Diamond Classics*, well-printed little books in 32mo and 48mo sizes. The series included the works of Shakespeare, Homer, Virgil, and Dante. Several of the volumes were bound in what is believed to be the earliest form of publisher's cloth.

In 1829 Pickering formed an active association in the production of fine books with Charles Whittingham the Younger, an association that lasted until Pickering's death in 1854. In 1830 Pickering began to issue the "Aldine Edition" of the *British Poets*, fifty-three volumes, completed in 1845. The publication marked the adoption by Pickering of the dolphin-and-anchor device of Aldus Manutius (*q.v.*), to which he added the inscription "Aldi Discipulus Anglus." Among the many fine books published by Pickering mention must be made of his splendid reprints of the *Book of Common Prayer* of 1549, 1552, 1559, 1604, 1637, 1662, and 1837. The seven volumes were issued in 1844.

picking A defect in presswork resulting in the lifting of paper particles.

pickup Composed type matter which has been kept standing since its first use and which can be "picked up" for further use.

pie; pi Type accidentally mixed up, or "knocked into pie."

pigskin The tough and strong skin of a pig, used in binding. The graining can be easily distinguished from the graining of morocco by the little hair punctures that show on the surface.

pin seal *See* seal.

piracy; pirate In the book industry, piracy is the production or publishing of a book without permission of the copyright owner; a pirate is the offending party; to pirate is to commit piracy. In recent times, book pirates have been numerous, primarily in Asia, where, in several countries, local proprietors of small offset lithography shops have copied Western text, reference, and popular books for sale at prices more within their customers' means than imported editions. Authorization of reprints at low or merely token royalties has grown as one answer to this practice; development and enforcement of national copyright laws is another answer. *See also* Universal Copyright Convention.

planography One of the four basic principles of printing, the others being relief, intaglio, and screen process. Lithography (*q.v.*) or offset is a planographic process as is photogelatin. In planography the printing areas and the nonprinting areas are in the same plane, neither raised nor depressed. Inking is possible because the printing areas are made chemically ink-receptive and the nonprinting areas are made ink-repellent.

plant A publisher's designation for a printer's establishment.

Plantin, Christophe (1520?–1589) The greatest of all printers at Antwerp. He was a Frenchman, born near Tours. After serving an apprenticeship as a printer, he set up a shop in Paris in 1546. Two years later he gave it up and moved to Antwerp where he opened a shop and sold books, prints, and tooled leather. In 1555 he began a publishing business which flourished, and by 1570 his establishment became one of the most celebrated of the time. He was appointed court printer to Philip II of Spain, and his large plant employed over 150 workmen.

The most noted of all his fine publications is the great Polyglot Bible, *Biblia Sacra: Hebraice, Chaldice, Graece & Latine* (8 volumes, 1569–1572). Eminent French type designers, notably Granjon and Garamond, prepared special types for this work, which is unrivalled as printer's achievement.

Upon Plantin's death in 1589 the business passed to his son-in-law Jean Moretus, and it was carried on by the Moretus family in the original Plantin house until 1876, when the city of Antwerp and the Belgian government united to purchase it as a public museum. All of the records of the business, the fonts of type, the cases with wood blocks and metal cuts, etc., are here preserved, making this museum the most significant and instructive of printing meccas.

plastic binding *See* binding.

platen press A style of printing press in which the paper rests on a flat surface known as the platen, and is forced against the printing image carrier, which is positioned on another flat surface known as the bed. Cf. flat-bed cylinder press; rotary press.

plates (1) Illustrations printed separately and inserted in a book when bound. (2) The master surfaces from which printing is done, such as electrotype plates, stereotype plates, engraved plates, offset lithographic plates, rubber plates, plastic plates, photogelatin plates, gravure plates, etc.

plug (1) Trade term for an unsaleable book; also known as *dog, turkey, stiff, bomb.* (2) To "plug" a book is to try to win friends for it.

pochoir The French word for stencil. A stencil process similar to *silk screen (q.v.),* except that paper stencils are often used and the color is daubed through rather than drawn across the open areas of the stencil. Pochoir cannot reproduce such letters as the O and A in one operation without the use of disfiguring bridges which hold the stencil together. The process permits the use of watercolor inks with an unpolished finish not obtained by colors printed under pressure. Extensively used in France.

pocket part A supplement to a law book, brought out to update the book, and kept in a pocket provided at the back of the book.

point (1) In book collecting, a feature, typographical or other, by which states or issues in an edition may be distinguished. (2) In type, *see* American point system.

point system *See* American point system.

pointillé A form of gilt decoration on bookbindings in which scrolls and other ornaments consist of dotted lines instead of solid lines. This style was used with great effect by the seventeenth century binder Le Gascon (*q.v.*).

polyglot (1) One who speaks or writes several languages. (2) A book containing versions of the same text in several languages—especially the Scriptures in several languages.

   Three famous polyglot Bibles are: the *Complutensian Polyglot* (also called the Ximenes Polyglot, after Cardinal Ximenes, its patron), printed 1513–17 at Complutum (now Alcalá de Henares); the *Antwerp Polyglot,* or *Biblia Regia,* published by Christophe Plantin, at Antwerp, 1569–72; and the *London,* or *Walton's Polyglot Bible,* edited by Brian Walton, Bishop of Chester, and issued in 1654–57.

popular copyrights An expression which came into use at the turn of the century when publishers of low-priced editions began to reprint popular books from the plates and with the permission of the copyright owners.

pornography From the Greek, meaning "writing about harlots"; originally applied only to treatises on prostitutes and prostitution. Currently describes writings of an obscene or licentious character. Sometimes catalogs of books include such items under the terms *erotica, curiosa,* or *facetiae* (*qq.v.*).

port.   Abbreviation for portrait.

positive   *See* negative.

Pott octavo   *See* book sizes.

pre-pub   Abbreviation of pre-publication, denoting a special price or terms offered before the stated publication date of a book.

prebinding   *See* binding.

preface   A short explanatory note by the author preceding the text of a book and usually touching on the purpose of the book, its sources, extent, etc. *Foreword* (*q.v.*) often has the same scope as preface but is written by someone other than the author. An *introduction*, however, forms part of the work itself.

The preface affords the author an opportunity to speak to his reader in a comparatively direct and personal manner, and to acquaint him with the considerations which impelled the author to write the book. At the end of a preface it is customary for the author to acknowledge the services of those who assisted him in writing the book, or who helped in reading the proofs, or who contributed information, etc. *See also* front matter.

prelims.   Abbreviation for preliminary pages, meaning *front matter* (*q.v.*).

preprints   Copies of a book or sections of a book or periodical, usually paperbound, issued in limited number and for some special purpose before publication day.

presentation copy   A book with a presentation inscription by the author. *See also* association books.

press errors   Mistakes made by the compositor in setting type.

press proofs   *See* proofs.

press queries   Queries to the author marked on proofs by the printer's proofreader.

press-ready   *See* make-ready.

press run   Number of copies to be printed, usually larger (to allow for spoilage) than the binding order.

presswork   That part of the printing process that concerns the running of the paper through the printing press. The three major steps in printing a book are: composition, presswork, and binding.

printer   In computers, an output device for producing the results of computer processing on paper.

printer's error   *See* misprint.

printer's flower   *See* floret.

printer's mark   The device of a printer for the identification of his product. *See also* colophon.

printing-image carrier   A generic term for the wide variety of intermediate products needed for image transfer or presswork. Printing-image carriers are the result of the image conversion process beginning with original art and copy. Among them are type forms, various kinds of offset plates, rotogravure cylinders, screen process screens, curved stereotype and electrotype plates, flexographic rubber and plastic plates, and many others.

printing presses   Machines equipped for producing the final printed images by inking the printing-image carrier (*q.v.*) and transferring the ink image, directly or indirectly, onto the paper or other printing stock. In sheet-fed presses the printed sheets are piled prior to removal from the press; in roll-fed presses, the web may be sheeted, or folded, or otherwise processed. Printing presses are available in a vast variety.

printout   A record on paper of the results of a computer's computations and processing. *See also* printer.

private book clubs   *See* book-collectors' clubs.

private presses   Printing establishments which undertake only the work of the owner or of publishing clubs which may be supporting the press. As John T. Winterich defined it, "A private press is . . . an enterprise conceived, and masterfully and thoroughly carried out, by a creative artist who (whether or not he likes to cover some of his expenses by sales) does his work from a sincere conviction that he is so expressing his own personality." (From *Private Presses and their Books,* by Will Ransom, published 1929 by the R. R. Bowker Co.)

privately printed   In the antiquarian book trade, a cataloger's term for a work not published for sale. Also applied, loosely, to books issued from a private press, or books printed for private distribution only.

prizes   For complete information about literary prizes, refer to *Literary and Library Prizes* (Bowker, 1973).

process color   The technique used by printers to reproduce an infinite range of colors with a limited number of inks, sometimes called *four-color printing,* since very successful results are achieved with yellow, cyan, magenta, and black. These may be combined to reproduce all of the grays, browns, greens, purples, oranges, tints, etc., that may be in the original art work. Successful results are often achieved in gravure with only three colors, the black being omitted. More than four colors may also be used. *See also* color printing. The term *color separation* is given to the procedures by which a full-color original is photographed or scanned through color filters that will sort out all the yellows for one plate, all the cyan components for another, etc.

processing section   The part of a computer that does the actual work on data. *See also* central processing unit.

program   (1) The complete set of instructions in machine language which directs the computer to perform each operation at the right time in proper sequence. (2) The act of writing a program.

programmer   One who writes a program.

programming   The process of writing a program.

progressive proofs   Proofs of plates for color printing, showing each color separately and also the combined colors in the order they are to print (second on first; third on second and first; and fourth on third, second and first).

projected books   Microfilmed books intended for projecting on a ceiling or screen for the benefit of physically handicapped persons.

proofreader   Person who reads printer's proof against the "copy" from which it was set for correction of errors.

proofreaders' marks   *See* end of book.

proofs; proof sheets   Trial prints from type, plates, or cylinders, etc. Proofs required of matter set in type for publication in book form are successively: (1) *galley proofs* (*q.v.*); (2) page proofs, with galley corrections made and set up in page form; (3) foundry proofs, if duplicate plates are to be made; (4) stone proofs, made after the form has been locked up for press, but before it is put on the press; (5) press proofs, made on the printing press just prior to starting the run. When engravings are made, engravers' proofs are supplied and used for checking the quality of the work and for dummying up in pages. For offset, gravure, and photogelatin, page proofs of type are followed by reproduction proofs (perfect proofs intended to be photographed) and blueprint or vandyke prints may be made prior to making the final plate.

prospectus   A descriptive circular used in soliciting orders, sometimes including a sample page or illustration.

protection   The policy by which a publisher may permit booksellers to return unsold books to him for credit. The increasingly more common term for this is *returns policy*; *see* returns.

provenance   A record of ownership of a book or manuscript.

pseudonym   An assumed name or nom de plume.

public domain (in the)   Not protected by copyright.

publication date   The date a book becomes available to the public. Trade publishers endeavor to have their books in the stores when the reviews break, which means sending out review copies and starting the promotion and distribution process weeks or months ahead of the "publication date." Books that are not dependent on attention from daily or weekly reviewers may not have formal publication dates, being assumed to be "published" the day the bindery starts shipping.

publisher   One who issues or causes to be issued books, periodicals, music, maps, or the like. Publishing as a business apart from bookselling developed about the middle of the nineteenth century.

The publisher's functions consist of: selecting the manuscript; acquiring publishing rights; editing the manuscript; having the type set; ordering, purchasing or leasing the plates; designing the format; arranging for the purchase of paper and other materials, and for printing and binding the book; promoting and advertising the book; using an imprint to identify him as publisher on the title page, spine, and jacket of the book; distributing the book; arranging for sales of subsidiary rights; paying royalties to the author; generally undertaking the ultimate risk of the venture as entrepreneur.

publishers' binding   The ordinary trade binding of a book as distinguished from bindings made to special order.

Publishers Weekly   Journal of the American book industry, founded in 1872. Provides current news and reports on trends, companies, persons, business activities and methods, in all areas of the business and profession of books; features extensive listings and reviews of forthcoming books. Published by the R. R. Bowker Company. *See also* Richard Rogers Bowker; Frederick Leypoldt; Frederic G. Melcher.

pull-case   A protective box for books, pamphlets, etc., which telescopes. *See also* slip-case; solander.

pulls   An English term for *proofs* (*q.v.*).

pulp   (1) The mixture of water and fiber from which paper is made. Fiber used is usually taken from wood or rags or a mixture of both, but may be from straw, bark, or any fibrous material. *See also* chemical pulp; groundwood pulp; rag paper. (2) A magazine printed on paper made of groundwood pulp (newsprint). *See also* slick.

punch card   A standard-size card in which holes are punched to encode data for entry into a computer.

punch tape   Synonym for perforated tape.

Pynson, Richard (d. 1530)   Norman by birth; took over the printing business of William de Machlinia in England in 1490; moved to Fleet Street in London in 1500. Appointed Royal Printer to Henry VIII in 1508. Introduced roman type into England in 1509 using it for the first time in *Sermo Fratris Hieronymi de Ferraria*. Considered to be the outstanding printer of his day in England.

pyroxylin   Plastic material (cellulose nitrate) used for impregnating or coating book cloth.

quad   Metal blank used for filling spaces in typesetting; abbreviated from "quadrat," a square. The em quad (so called because it occupies about the same space as a capital M) is a common unit of measurement and spacing. An en quad is half the width of an em quad. Quads are also cast in two-em and three-em lengths.

quadding   Positioning of type lines horizontally either flush to the left margin, centered or flush to the right margin.

quality or trade paperbacks   Higher-priced paperbound books frequently published by the same publishers who produce hardbound trade books, and marketed through the normal book trade channels. *See also* mass-market paperbacks.

quarter-binding   *See* binding.

quarto (4to)   *See* book sizes.

query   A marginal note in copy or on proofs, to call attention to some matter in doubt.

quire   (1) A little-used paper term, a printer's quire being twenty-four sheets. The term is uncommon in the book industry but is still used by stationers. (2) A *signature* (*q.v.*). *See also* in quires.

quoins   Wedges used to lock up type pages in the chase.

r.p.n.d.   Abbreviation for "reprinting, no date."

rag-content paper   *See* linen paper.

rag paper   Paper made from cotton or linen rags. Many fine writing or book papers are sold as one hundred percent rag, or as having a rag content of twenty-five, fifty, or seventy-five percent. Rag paper can withstand many folds before tearing, but proof is lacking that it has any more permanence than paper made from wood by the chemical pulp process. *See* chemical pulp.

random access storage A storage technique which enables data stored at any location in the memory to be retrieved about as quickly as data stored at any other location, as opposed to sequential storage which often requires searching through a long string of data to find that desired. *See also* sequential storage.

rarity The degrees of rarity are as infinite as the needs of antiquarian bookmen. John Carter's chapters on "rarity" and "condition" in "Taste and Technique in Book-Collecting" should be required reading for every bookman. The following terms were proposed as basic by *Antiquarian Bookman:*

Unique: characterization of an item when no other copy is known or recorded.

Extremely rare: examples turn up in a specialist's hands but once in a lifetime.

Rare: examples turn up in a specialist's hands but once in a decade.

Scarce: examples turn up in a specialist's hands but once in a year.

Ratdolt, Erhard (1442?–1528) German printer and typecutter, born at Augsburg. Printed at Venice between 1476 and 1486; returned to Augsburg in 1487 and was printer there until his death.

At Venice, Ratdolt was in partnership with Peter Loeslein and Bernhard Maler. They produced decorated books by typographical methods, and were among the first to print in several colors on one page. Their printing of Johann Mueller's *Kalendarium* of 1476 is the earliest book to contain a complete decorative title page.

raw data Data that has not been acted upon by the computer.

raw tape Synonym for idiot tape.

read In computer processing, the function of sensing and putting into a computer or section of a computer.

read-out The process of sensing data within a computer or section of a computer and transmitting it out to another location, such as external memory or a printout device.

reader One who reads manuscripts for a publisher or literary agent and reports on the advisability of publishing them. A "first reader" is the one who first screens the manuscripts coming into the publishing house, selecting those that may deserve at least one more scanning.

reader's set The set of proofs on which corrections are to be made, usually so marked on the proofs by the printer.

reading circle (1) An organization for the cooperative buying of books other than textbooks for schools and school libraries. (2) A group of persons, especially in Europe, who purchase books for circulation among themselves.

real time Performance of computer operations within the time span required to perform related physical processes, so that the computer operations do not limit or slow down a person working with the system.

ream A standard parcel of paper, formerly twenty quires or 480 sheets, now usually 500 sheets. Handmade and drawing papers may contain 472, 480, or 500 sheets.

   The unit of quantity now adopted by many American paper dealers is 1,000 sheets, thus doing away with the ream as a basis of count. In England the standard basis is also 1,000 sheets. Basis weight, however, is still expressed on a 500-sheet ream basis. *See also* basis weight.

rebacked A volume repaired by replacing the old spine with a new one.

recased The sheets of a book rebound in its original covers, in the covers of another copy of the same title, or in a new case.

recto A right-hand page of a book; also the front of a separate printed sheet. The left-hand page and the reverse of a printed sheet is the *verso*.

red under gold A method of treating the edges of a book by staining them red and gilding over the stain. Frequently used on Bibles, prayer books, dictionaries, etc. Occasionally used in printing illustrations, as in the Greek medallions in the original Lawrence *Odyssey*, designed by Bruce Rogers.

reference marks Printers' marks used to indicate references to other books or passages, or to footnotes on the page. When more than one reference is given on a page, the order of the marks is as follows: * (asterisk), † (dagger), ‡ (double dagger), § (section), ‖ (parallel), ¶ (paragraph). If necessary, the series is repeated, using two of each mark in the same order. Superior figures (*q.v.*) are more often used for the same purpose.

register (1) Correct position on the sheet. In book work accurate register means keeping to the specified margins, a good test being to see whether the work on an even-numbered (left) page exactly backs the preceding type page. In color work with more than one plate accurate register is essential. When there is a faulty adjustment the printing is said to be "off register" or "out of register." (2) The register (in its use in incunabula) is a list of the signatures often given at the end of early books, especially those printed in Italy. Its purpose is to indicate to the binder the order and number of the gatherings.

reglet A thin wooden strip used for spacing between units of type matter. *See also* leads.

reissue (1) A reprint of a published work from the type, plates, or film of the original edition. In the mass-market paperback trade, a reissue is a new printing from a previous edition, often with a new cover design. (2) In bibliography, according to Gaskell, *A New Introduction to Bibliography*, "Reissue normally involves a new or altered title-page, and includes cases such as: the cancellation of the title-page to bring old sheets up to date; a new impression with a new title-page; and collections of separate pieces with a new general title."*

rejection slip A printed slip sent out by a publisher with a returned manuscript informing the author that the manuscript will not be used for publication.

relief printing A generic term for all kinds of printing, letterpress in particular, in which the printing area is in relief, above the supporting material. Other examples of relief printing are flexography which uses rubber plates, newspaper relief printing from curved stereotyped or plastic plates, and in a sense, rubber stamping.

remainder dealers Specialists in purchasing remainders (*q.v.*) from publishers.

remainders Publishers' overstocks of titles whose sale has slackened, offered at reduced price through jobbers and booksellers. *See also* partial remaindering.

remake To repage a book, completely or partly; to rearrange typographic elements in a page or publication.

remote station Input-output device located some distance from the computer, usually connected to the system by wire in an on-line mode, but not necessarily.

rental library A collection of books, usually current fiction, for lending at a rental fee for a stated period. Also known as *circulating* or *lending library*.

reprint (1) A new printing of a book. (2) A term used for an edition in cheaper form than the original and often issued by another publisher who specializes in such popular editions.

repro Camera-ready copy to be photographed in preparation for making printing plates. Short for reproduction proof.

---

*Gaskell, Philip. *A New Introduction to Bibliography*. © 1972 Oxford University Press. Reproduced by permission of The Clarendon Press, Oxford.

reproduction proofs *See* proofs.

reprography A wide range of printing and reproduction processes used mainly internally in companies and other organizations for quick-service duplicating needs. Processes include diazo, xerography, offset lithography, and microfilming.

resetting Setting type again, because of corrections, additions, etc.

resolution The ability to render or retain fine detail in an image that has been processed photographically. A measure of such an image's quality.

retouching Modifying or improving artwork or a printing plate by hand.

returns Unsold books returned for cash or credit to the publisher. The publisher's stated terms under which he does this constitutes his returns policy. *See also* protection.

reversal processing In photography, the production of a positive from a positive copy or a negative from a negative copy, through a special chemical process.

review copies Gratis copies of a newly published work sent out by its publisher for review, notice, or record. *See also* advance copies.

revise Any proof taken after an earlier proof has been read and corrections made. *See* proof.

revised edition A book that has been reissued with changes from the original or previous edition.

right-reading A film image in which the type reads from left to right and top to bottom when the emulsion side faces the viewer. *See also* wrong-reading

rights Rights to a literary property include the following: pre-publication serial (first serial rights); book publication, including book club; magazine second serial; newspaper second serial; book reprint; dramatization; dramatization for stock; musical comedy; amateur leasing; motion picture (commercial and non-commercial); radio; television; mechanical, electronic, or xerographic reproduction, or other kinds covered in the inclusive term "reprographic reproduction"; condensation and abridgment; anthology; translation; quotation; commercial exploitation rights. Most of these are also commonly referred to as *subsidiary rights.*

Rittenhouse, William (1644–1708) Mennonite clergyman and industrialist. Born in Muelheim, Prussia; emigrated to America in 1688 and settled in Germantown, Pa.; chosen first pastor of the Mennonite group there; elected bishop (1703) of the first Mennonite church in America.

In 1690 he organized a paper-manufacturing company, and in partnership with Samuel Carpenter, William Bradford, and others, he built the first paper mill in America.

river   A streak of white space in printed matter resulting from the fact that the spaces between words in several lines happen to occur almost one below the other.

roan   An inexpensive binding leather, made of sheepskin.

Rogers, Bruce (1870–1957)   Distinguished American printer and designer of fine typography. He first gained attention by his book designs of the limited editions issued at the Riverside Press between 1900 and 1911. A year's association with Carl Purington Rollins at Rollins's private press, in Montague, Mass., produced, among other works, the famous edition of Maurice de Guerin's *The Centaur*, 1915, in the translation by George B. Ives, set in Rogers' new Centaur type. There followed work in London with Sir Emery Walker, and at the Cambridge University Press; then at Harvard University Press, the Rudge Press, and Oxford University Press. His Homer, *The Odyssey*, 1932, in the translation by T. E. Shaw [Lawrence]; his Oxford Lectern Bible, 1935; and the Bible designed in 1949 for the World Publishing Company, rank among his most notable books.

Rollins, Carl Purington (1880–1960)   One of America's eminent book designers. In 1909 he established the Montague Press (at Montague, Mass.), a small private press which became known for the quality of its output. In 1918 he joined the Yale Press, and from 1920 to 1948 he was Printer to Yale University. *See also* Rogers, Bruce.

rom.   Abbreviation for *roman* (*q.v.*).

roman   A style of lettering developed about 1500, south of the Alps where early type designers followed the rough humanistic handwriting of the scribes of that section.

Roman numerals   *See* numerals, Roman.

Rosenbach, Abraham S. W. (1876–1952)   Bibliophile and antiquarian bookseller who served as counselor and bookbuyer for famous American book collectors of his time.

rotary press   A style of press that prints from the curved plates held on a cylinder; the most efficient style of press for fast and long-run presswork. The printing units consist of two, three, or more cylinders. In direct printing these are the plate cylinder and the impression cylinder; in indirect, or offset printing, a blanket cylinder is added.

The image carriers for rotary presses vary according to many considerations. High-quality letterpress uses mainly curved electrotypes; rubber and plastic plates are used in flexography and on the belt press; newspaper relief printing prefers curved-cast stereotype plates or plastic plates. Offset lithography uses a whole range of thin plates, from paper for short runs to steel for very long ones. Rotogravure, finally, does not employ plates, but etched cylinders.

Rotary presses, in many sizes and styles are made for: printing of sheets and rolls, printing in one or more colors in one pass through the press, and printing the sheet or web on one or on both sides in various color combinations. Some web presses are equipped to fold and cut the printed paper into units of different sizes; some are connected to fabricating equipment.

rotogravure   *See* gravure.

rounding   In binding, the process of curving and fanning out the back of a book into a rounded shape by rubbing the binding edges of sheets or signatures with rounded irons. The process gives a book a convex spine and a concave fore-edge and makes the back wider than the rest of the book so that the spine will wrap around the edges of the cover boards at the joint. Rounding is done after sewing (or gluing in adhesive binding) and before backing.

routine   In a computer, a set of procedures to be performed in proper sequence. *See also* subroutine.

routing   Cutting away that part of any letterpress printing block which is not needed, and which would be likely to catch ink and thus leave a blemish on the sheet.

roxburghe   A style of binding with a plain roan back, cloth or board sides, gilt top and other edges untrimmed. The style was used for the publications of the Roxburghe Club, a private book collectors' club, founded in London in 1812, and named for the Third Duke of Roxburghe.

royal octavo; royal quarto   *See* book sizes.

royalties   A compensation paid by the publisher to the author or owner of a copyright for the right to act under it, usually on the basis of a percentage of the list price of the book on each copy sold, but sometimes paid on a percentage of the wholesale price or on the publisher's total receipts. No royalty is paid on review copies or on copies sold out as remainders. A lower rate is paid on reprints, book club editions, and many scholarly works, and sometimes on copies sold by mail order or exported.

rub-out code   A code used to cancel out previously encoded data in a perforated paper tape.

rubbed   A cataloging term in the antiquarian book trade, indicating that the binding of the item listed shows signs of chafing.

rubric   The heading of a chapter or other division of a book, printed in red ink, with the rest of the text printed in black.

rules   Strips of brass or type metal used to print lines and borders.

run   A single processing of data by a computer under control of a program.

run-around   When some of the lines in a column of type are shortened to allow a cut or other featured material to appear within the text area, such treatment is called a "run-around."

run in   Direction to set composed matter without a paragraph or break; to make one paragraph of two or more.

run on   When the printing press is allowed to continue, after the budgeted printing is completed, the extra copies so produced can be figured at a cost of nothing but paper, press time, and binding, and are said to be produced at "run on cost."

running head   The line which appears across the top of a printed page. Usually the title of the book appears on the left-hand page and the chapter title on the right-hand page. Running heads may be omitted altogether.

Russia leather   A high-grade binding leather, now made from various skins, though originally made in Russia from the hides of young cattle. Besides the tanning, it is treated with birch oil, which gives it its characteristic odor and protects it from insects. It is usually colored red with brazilwood.

SAN   *See* Standard Account Number.

SBN   See International Standard Book Number.

sc   (1) Abbreviation for small caps. (2) Abbreviation for super-calendered paper.

s.c.o.p.   Abbreviation for "single copy order plan" (*q.v.*).

SLA   *See* Special Libraries Association.

STC   *See* Short-Title Catalogue.

Sabin, Joseph   (1821–1881) Bibliographer, bookseller, cataloger, and auctioneer of books, was born in Branston, England, in 1821. He came to the United States in 1848 and engaged in bookselling and bibliographical work in Philadelphia and New York. He opened his Nassau Street bookshop in New York in 1864, and he became one of the leading booksellers in the city. He compiled the catalogs of many important book auction sales, and served as book auctioneer at the house of George A. Leavitt & Company.

After his death in 1881 Sabin became better known as a bibliographer and distinguished expert of American books than as a rare book dealer. His great work, and that which gives him undying fame, was his *Dictionary of Books Relating to America, from its Discovery to the Present Time* (also known by its original half-title, *Bibliotheca Americana*), which during his lifetime he finished to the letter "O." After Sabin's death the work was continued by Wilberforce Eames, and completed by Robert W. G. Vail.

Of the total 172 parts (twenty-nine volumes), Sabin completed the first eighty-two parts (volumes 1–14, printed 1868 to 1884); parts 83 to 116 were done by Wilberforce Eames (volumes 15–20, printed 1885 to 1892). The work was dormant from 1893 to 1924. In 1925 Miss Elizabeth G. Greene, and in 1927 Miss Marjorie Watkins joined Dr. Eames as his assistants, and the work was resumed with part 117, printed in 1927. R. W. G. Vail headed an enlarged staff in 1927–29; in 1930 he became joint editor, and the printing of the *Bibliotheca Americana* was completed with part 172 of the twenty-ninth and last volume of the work, issued in 1936. The title page of volume 29 carries the statement: "Begun by Joseph Sabin, continued by Wilberforce Eames, and Completed by R. W. G. Vail for the Bibliographical Society of America."

"Sabin" is the most comprehensive reference work relating to Americana. 106,413 numbered entries are given, but the actual number of titles recorded is much greater as that total does not count the added editions and titles mentioned in the various notes.

In November 1973 an announcement was made by The Whitston Publishing Company, Troy, N.Y. 12181, of the publication of the first volume of *THE NEW SABIN; Books Described by Joseph Sabin and His Successors, Now Described Again, on the Basis of Examination of Originals, and Fully Indexed by Title, Subject, Joint Authors . . .* Edited by Lawrence S. Thompson, Professor of Classics, University of Kentucky.

saddle sewing   *See* sewing.

saddle stitching   *See* stitching.

saddle-wire stitching   *See* stitching.

salesman   *See* traveler.

sample pages   Selected pages of a prospective book, set by the printer in accordance with the designer's specifications and used as a model for setting the entire book.

sans serif   A style of typeface distinguished by the absence of serifs or "ticks" on the ends of strokes and by the absence of any pronounced variations in the thickness of the stroke. Originally known as gothic. Two modern examples of sans serif are Futura and Gill. *See also* serif; gothic.

Sauer [Sower], Christopher (1693–1758) Born near Marburg, Hesse; emigrated to Philadelphia in 1724; set up as a farmer in Lancaster; established himself in Germantown in 1731, where he dealt in imported German theological treatises. Took up printing on his own account and in 1735 he issued the first German almanac to be published in the colonies. In 1743 he printed an edition of the Bible in German (Martin Luther's translation), the first Bible in a European language printed in the colonies.

Christopher Sauer the Younger (1721–1784) continued the business, but in 1778 he was arrested on suspicion of treason and all of his property was confiscated; the sheets that were on hand of the German Bible he had printed in 1776 were converted into gun-wadding by the American troops, and that edition came to be known as the "Gun-Wad Bible."

scaling The process of calculating and indicating how an illustration is to be cropped and how much it must be enlarged or reduced to fit into the layout.

scanner A device for sensing the presence or absence of data on various surfaces presented to it, such as magnetic tapes or disks or printed sheets. *See also* optical character recognition.

Schoeffer, Peter (1425?–1502) *See* Fust, Johann.

Schuster, Max Lincoln (1898–1971) Editor and publisher of books of quality, designed for large sale. With Robert L. Simon he founded Simon and Schuster in 1924. Schuster's flood of ideas for books of lively educational value combined with popular appeal and tasteful typography was a key to the firm's influence. The firm also set high standards of pictorial and production excellence in low-cost, mass-merchandised books, especially children's books.

science fiction Imaginative fiction describing life in the future, interplanetary travel, life on other worlds, and the like. It is usually distinguished by having a scientific or prophetic background, or both. Also called science fantasy; and often related to but usually distinct from fantasy fiction or fantastic fiction.

scoring Compressing the fiber of paper along a line either to facilitate folding or to facilitate tearing. Done on either a regular printing press, a special cutting and creasing press, or a folding machine by impressing a raised rule or disk against the paper. Scoring with a dull rule (also called *creasing*) actually increases the folding endurance. Scoring with a sharp rule partially breaks the paper fibers and is similar in its effect to perforating.

scout A person engaged by the editorial department of a publishing house to look for new and promising writers and to explore ideas for new books. *See also* book scout.

script A typeface having some characteristics of handwriting.

screen (1) The implement for converting continuous-tone images into halftones. (2) The implement for providing the support of the doctor blade in most methods of rotogravure. (3) The printing-image carrier in screen printing. All three points denote different objects; which of them is meant depends on the general context in which the term is used. (4) In a computer system, the face of a cathode-ray tube on which images are displayed. *See also* cathode-ray tube.

scroll (1) A roll of papyrus or parchment, and also, later, of paper. (2) A writing formed into a roll, such as the engrossed proceedings of a public body or a court.

seal Leather made from the skin of the seal, with a coarse grain, soft to the touch. Pin seal is from the skin of the very young or baby seal, having a much finer grain and a lustrous finish.

search In a computer, to match coded data in memory against specified criteria, also coded, to find items desired.

search service Business of searching for out-of-print books that are wanted by customers. The service may be conducted by a regular dealer in old and rare books, or by a specialized searcher who advertises his services and obtains orders by mail.

secretary shift The type of keyboard shift control which automatically reverts to the unshift condition when the shift button is released, eliminating the need for a separate unshift keystroke.

section *See* signature.

see copy In proof correction, a direction to the printer to compare the marked passage with the original copy, when there appears to be a discrepancy.

self-wrapper The printed or unprinted paper cover of a pamphlet or book. A self-wrapper, as opposed to *wrapper* or *wrappers* (*q.v.*), is an integral part of the sheet or sheets comprising the body of a publication so bound. For example, the self-wrapper of a sixteen-page pamphlet, printed in octavo, would be the first and last leaves printed as part of the body of the publication and not a binder's addition.

Senefelder, Alois (1771–1834) The inventor of lithography (*q.v.*).

separation negatives Individual negatives for each color used in reproducing art work. *See also* process color.

sequence The order in which operations are to be performed in a computer.

sequential card system A composing system in which cards containing copy to be photographed are placed in the order they are to appear in the publication. Then the camera unit photographs each card at high speed, forming columns of typeset copy or even pages in some cases. Later, cards are filed and held for the next edition, and updated in the meantime.

sequential storage Storage of data in a linear mode, such as a string of codes on tape, as opposed to random-access storage. Sequential storage often is less expensive than random-access storage, but it also usually takes more time to find data. *See also* random-access storage.

ser. In cataloging, abbreviation for series.

serial A publication issued in successive parts, usually at regular intervals, and intended to be continued indefinitely. Serials include periodicals, annuals, and proceedings and transactions of societies.

serial rights *See* rights.

series Separate and successive publications on a given subject, having a collective series title and uniform format, and usually all issued by the same publisher.

serif A finishing line or stroke crossing or projecting from the end of a main line or stroke in a letter, as at the top and bottom of the letter M. Gothic or sans serif letters (**M**) have no serifs.

service basis A method of pricing on a sliding scale, as determined by the library budget, or by some other criteria.

set Type is set by being assembled into words, lines, paragraphs, and so on. *See also* set size.

set-off In presswork, the unwanted transfer of incompletely dried ink from one sheet to another.

set size The width of type across the character. The set width of a given typeface can be varied within limits on the Monotype and on most photocomposing machines, but not on the Linotype. Different typefaces of the same point size normally have different set sizes (or widths). For example, because a typeface such as Granjon, has a narrower set size than, say, Bodoni, it permits more characters to be fitted into a given length line. Sometimes referred to as the set of a type.

set solid   A direction to the printer to set the lines of type without leads between.

set width   *See* set size.

sewing   The method of holding pages and signatures of a book together by means of thread. The terms sewing and stitching are sometimes used interchangeably, but the preference today among binders is to use sewing to indicate thread binding and stitching to indicate wire-staple binding.

Within these definitions, there are a number of forms of sewing. Saddle sewing fastens a set of folded sheets such as a signature together by sewing through the folded edges. Smyth sewing links side-by-side signatures by saddle sewing with a continuous thread through the folded edges of one signature after another, fastening each signature to the next. Side sewing passes thread through the side of the book along the binding edge. Oversewing, which is used in library rebinding, sews loose leaves together, in small groups, with an overlapping series of stitches across the spine of the book. Cleat sewing, a relatively new method, is a mechanized version of the basic hand-sewing method; cleats or notches are cut in the backbone of the book and adhesive-coated thread is passed around the projections and through the pages. McCain and Singer sewing, named after the machines used, actually are versions of the above processes. Singer sewing can be either side or saddle sewing, and McCain sewing is side sewing. All of these are machine processes; custom bound books are sometimes still sewed by hand.

In the nineteenth century, sewing and stitching had substantially different meanings than they do now. Jacob Abbott in 1855 in *The Harper Establishment* says, "If the work is a pamphlet . . . it is stitched. If it is a bound book, it is to be sewed. To prepare the pamphlet for stitching, three holes are made through the sheets by means of a machine called a stabbing machine. . . . Books that are to be bound are sewed, as it is called; this is quite a different process from stitching. To prepare the books for being sewed, the first step is to saw small grooves through the backs . . . to receive the bands of twine to which each sheet is secured. . . ." *See also* stitching.

shaken   In cataloging, a term used to describe books in publisher's cloth, the inner hinges of which have become weak or torn.

shaved   A book trimmed so closely that the top or bottom lines of type on the pages have been grazed. *See also* crop.

sheet-feed   Said of a printing press which takes paper previously cut into separate sheets, as opposed to paper in a continuous roll.

sheets   Printed pages of a book, either flat or folded, but unbound; individual cut pieces of paper, fabric, or other material.

sheetwise   The process of printing the two sides of a sheet from two different forms, in contradistinction to *work and turn* (*q.v.*).

shelfback   *See* backbone.

shift-unshift codes   Special function codes which expand the capacity of a keyboard to produce codes. In the shift mode, a keyboard produces a different set of codes from those produced in the unshift mode. *See also* function code.

shingling   (1) "A method of making a column or page of type out of many separate cards or slips of paper, each containing one or a few lines of type. The type must be positioned near the edge of each card and the cards are then overlapped like shingles on a roof." (Daniel Melcher, from *Printing & Promotion Handbook*, Melcher & Larrick, McGraw-Hill Book Co.) (2) In saddle-stitched binding, a technique used when many leaves printed on heavy paper must be bound. The inside, or binding, margins are reduced in order to keep the printed pages provided with sufficiently wide trim margins.

short page   A shorter type page (*q.v.*) than has been specified.

Short-Title Catalogue   *A Short-Title Catalogue of Books printed in England, Scotland and Ireland, and of English Books printed Abroad, 1475–1640*. Compiled by Alfred W. Pollard and G. R. Redgrave (with the help of others). London, The Bibliographical Society, 1926 (and facsimile reprint, 1948).

A revised edition of this work, one of the most frequently quoted of reference books, is now (1974) nearing completion. More than ninety percent of the revision was accomplished by the late William A. Jackson, librarian of The Houghton Library, Harvard University, before his death in 1964.

Short-Title Catalogue of Books printed in England, Scotland, Ireland, Wales and British America, and of English Books printed in Other Countries, 1641–1700. Compiled by Donald Wing of the Yale University Library. New York, printed for The Index Society, 1945–48–51. 3 volumes. Published as a continuation of Pollard & Redgrave's *STC . . . 1475–1640*.

shorthand keyboarding   (1) A form of macro coding in which a single code is used to represent multiple codes. (2) Keyboard systems which use multiple keystrokes made simultaneously, as if playing a musical chord, to record data that would otherwise require a number of sequential keystrokes. *See also* macro code.

shorts   Items or quantities not in dealer's stock at the time an order is filled.

shoulder note   *See* marginalia.

side note   *See* marginalia.

side sewing   *See* sewing.

side sorts   Same as *odd sorts* (*q.v.*).

side stitching   *See* stitching.

side-wire stitching   *See* stitching.

sidehead   A heading set at the side of a page or column, either as a separate line set flush with the margin of the type page or run in with the paragraph to which it belongs.

signature   (1) A folded printed sheet forming one section of a book. A signature commonly has sixteen or thirty-two pages, although any multiple of four is possible. (*See* book sizes.) Sometimes called *gathering*, *quire*, or *section*. (2) The mark placed on the bottom of the first page, or on the outside fold of the signature, for the convenience of the binder in gathering.

silhouette   To remove nonessential background from a halftone cut to produce an outline effect.

silk screen printing   The major application (along with mimeographing) of the stencil principle of printing. Silk screen is little used for fine halftones or for small type, or for runs over 5,000–10,000 unless some of its specific effects are wanted. It is much used for posters and for printing on glass, plastics, and textured surfaces. It can be done as hand printing or by machines. A silk screen is a piece of stencil silk, plastic, or woven metal, stretched on a frame. The printing areas are left unblocked, the nonprinting areas are blocked and the design is transferred to the paper under the screen by pushing the ink across it and through the porous areas at the same time.

silked   *See* backed.

Singer sewing   *See* sewing.

Singer stitching   *See* sewing.

single copy order plan   A system devised and promoted by the American Booksellers' Association to maximize discount and minimize handling on single copy orders. Cooperating publishers grant full trade discount on single copies to dealers using the prescribed single copy order form available from the ABA.

sinkage   White space left at the top of a page, in addition to the regular top margins, as at the beginning of a new chapter.

sixteenmo (16mo); sixtyfourmo (64mo)   *See* book sizes.

sized   Paper is said to be sized when its surface has been treated to make it less receptive to water. Blotting paper is unsized. Writing paper is hard-sized. Offset lithographers prefer to work with paper that has been "sized for offset," to resist the moisture used in the process.

sizes of books   *See* book sizes.

skid   A quantity of sheet paper, usually about 3,000 pounds, varying with bulk and sheet size. The name comes from the movable wooden platforms (skids) on which the paper is delivered.

skiver   (1) Leather split with a knife. (2) The grain or hair side of a split sheepskin.

slander   Verbal (spoken) *libel* (*q.v.*).

slave   A device totally dependent on another device in a computer system for all its input data and any variable instructions required to operate it.

sleeper   (1) In the trade book field, a book for which there is apparently little initial demand, but for which a steady, often wide, market develops over a period of several months or a year. (2) In the rare book field, any item on a dealer's shelves or in a catalog which is marked at a very low price because the owner is unaware of its considerably higher monetary value.

slick   A magazine printed on slick paper. The word usually refers to a magazine carrying fiction for which the author is paid at a higher rate than is paid by the *pulps* (*q.v.*).

slip-case   A protective box-like container into which a book or books can be inserted. *See also* solander; pull-case.

slip-sheeting   Placing pieces of paper between printed sheets as they come from the press so that the printing on one sheet will set-off (*q.v.*), if at all, on the slip-sheet, not on another printed sheet.

slit-card   A poster slit so as to fit into or around a book for display purposes.

slitting   Cutting of paper into narrow ribbons or smaller sheets as it passes under special cutting wheels or disks on a regular printing press, a folder, or a special slitting machine.

slugs   (1) Pieces of lead, about ¾ inch high, and usually 6 or 12 points thick, used as spacing material between lines of type. (2) Lines of type in the form of metal bars as produced on the Linotype, Intertype, or Ludlow machines.

small caps   *See* caps and small caps.

smashing machine   Machine used in binderies for compressing folded signatures along the folds to render them more compact for binding.

Smyth sewing   *See* sewing.

soft copy   Images generated on the face of a cathode-ray tube, which will disappear when the data presented to the device for display changes, as opposed to hard copy which remains as a permanent record.

softcover   Another term for "paperback" or "paperbound."

software   Synonym for programming.

solander   A form of box, for keeping books and paper parts, pamphlets, illustrative plates, etc., which is shaped like a book and which opens like a book. The device was invented by Daniel Charles Solander, an eighteenth century botanist, for his specimens of flowers, etc. *See also* pull-case; slip-case.

solid matter   Type set without leads between the lines.

solid-state   A class of electronic components and devices made of semi-conductor materials, as opposed to the earlier vacuum tube technology.

sort   To arrange data in a specific sequence by application of rules.

sorts   In metal typesetting, a supplementary supply of characters with which to replenish the main supply.

Sower, Christopher   *See* Sauer, Christopher.

space dot   *See* centered dot.

spacebands   The wedge-shaped devices used on the Linotype and Intertype between words to permit justification of the line. In book work, narrow spacebands are often specified.

Spanish finish   *See* book cloth.

Special Libraries Association   International organization, founded in 1909, of professional librarians and information experts who serve all organizations, both public and private, requiring or providing specialized information. *See also* special library.

special library   A library maintained by a business firm, association, or other organization whose collections are limited in scope mainly to the subject areas of interest to the sponsoring organization. Special libraries serve manufacturing companies, banks, law firms, newspapers, advertising and insurance agencies, research organizations, museums, hospitals, and federal, state, and municipal government bureaus.

special order   To a bookseller, an order for a single copy of a book not in stock, handled at the customer's request. Because it requires special handling, and sometimes involves a short discount or no discount, the bookseller frequently adds a nominal service charge to the transaction to cover his trouble. *See also* single copy order plan.

special-purpose computer   A computer designed to accomplish one specific task or set of tasks, but not programmable for doing other kinds of work. *See also* general-purpose computer.

spine   *See* backbone.

spiral wire binding   *See* binding.

sponsored book   *See* subsidy publishing.

sprinkled edges   Book edges which, after being trimmed smooth, are spattered with color by means of a brush. Usually done on all three edges.

sq.   A catalog abbreviation describing the book as approximately square in shape.

stab marks   Punctures made in folded sheets of a book preparatory to sewing.

stabilization   A photographic development process in which the developing agents are embedded in the photographic paper.

stacks   Free-standing metal shelving, usually double-faced, holding the main body of the book collection in the library.

stained edges; stained top   The edges (or top) of a book stained with color. Staining helps prevent dust smudges or finger-marks from showing.

stamping   Pressing a design into a book cover using metal foil, colored foil, or ink, applied with brass or other dies. *See also* foil.

Standard Account Number (SAN)   A concise code for identification of bookdealers, libraries, schools, and school systems. Assignment of code numbers is centrally administered by the International Standard Book Numbering Agency. *See* International Standard Book Number.

Standard Book Number   *See* International Standard Book Number.

standing matter   Type matter held pending orders to print, reprint, or kill.

standing order   (1) An order which holds good until filled. (2) An order to supply each succeeding issue of an annual or serial. Also known as *continuation order.*

state   "The term *state* is used to cover all other variants from the basic form of the ideal copy. There are five major classes of variant state. (1) Alterations not affecting the make-up of the pages, made intentionally or unintentionally during printing, such as: stop-press corrections; resetting as the result of accidental damage to the type; resetting of distributed matter following a decision during printing to enlarge the edition quantity. (2) The addition, deletion, or substitution of matter, affecting the make-up of the pages, but carried out during printing. (3) Alterations made after some copies have been sold (not involving a new title page) such as the insertion or cancellation of preliminaries or text pages, or the addition of errata leaves, advertisements, etc. (4) Errors of imposition, or of machining (e.g., sheets perfected the wrong way round; but not errors of folding). (5) Special-paper copies not distinguished typographically from those on ordinary paper. . . .

"These terms are used with reference only to the printed sheets of a book, and are not affected by binding variants."*

Stationers' Company   The Company grew out of the fourteenth century guild of university *stationarii* (scribes and dealers in manuscripts); chartered as a guild in London in 1403. The official Charter of Incorporation was granted by Queen Mary in 1556 and confirmed by Queen Elizabeth in 1559. It constituted an organization of the printing and publishing trade of London to represent the publishing interests of the country. The hall of the Company, Stationers' Hall, in London, houses the register of copyright.

steel engraving   *See* engraving.

stencil   (1) The basic principle of printing underlying Mimeographing and silk screen printing (*q.v.*). In stencil printing the ink is applied to the back of the printing image carrier and reaches the front through the image areas which are porous or open. (2) The wax-impregnated master used in Mimeographing or Elliott addressing.

stencil work   *See* pochoir; silk screen printing.

stereotype plates; stereos   Letterpress duplicate plates made by molding type pages in a suitable material, forming a matrix. Molding is followed by casting, resulting in relief plates. Originally widely used for book printing, stereotypes are less used than electrotypes in long-run quality book work. Curved-cast stereotype plates are standard in many metropolitan newspapers. Some rubber and plastic plates are based on the stereotype principle, others on photomechanics.

stet   From the Latin verb "stare," to stand. When a word has been struck out in a proof and it is afterwards decided it should remain, the word is marked underneath with dots and *stet* written in the margin, meaning "let it stand."

stick *See* compose.

stipple engraving A method of hand engraving in which the effects are produced by dots instead of lines. *See also* mezzotint.

stitching The method of holding pages and signatures together by means of wire staples. The terms stitching and sewing are sometimes used interchangeably, but the preference today among binders is to use stitching to indicate wire-staple binding and sewing to indicate thread binding.

Within these definitions there are two basic types of stitching. Saddle stitching, sometimes called saddle-wire stitching, staples folded pages together by means of staples through the folded edge. This method is widely used for booklets and magazines. Side stitching, sometimes called side-wire stitching, is used for thicker books and publications. Here the staples are placed through the side of the book along the binding edge. *See also* sewing.

stone proofs *See* proofs.

storage Section of a computer system in which data is stored until needed. Storage devices within a computer usually are magnetic in nature, including cores, tapes, disks, and drums. Data also can be stored externally to the system on magnetic tapes or disks, or in the form of perforated paper tape, punch cards, or optically readable images. *See also* core storage; disk; pack; drum storage; perforated tape; punch card; tape.

stored-program computer A computer in which program instructions are stored in a section of memory and can be changed at any time, as opposed to a hard-wired computer in which programmed operations are permanently wired into the machine. *See also* hard-wired computer.

straight matter Type composition that does not contain display lines, formulas, tabular or other complicated matter.

Strawberry Hill Press Founded in 1757 by Sir Horace Walpole (1717–1797). The press was set up in a small cottage adjoining Walpole's villa at Twickenham. His first printer was William Robinson, who, following a dispute, was dismissed in 1759. Walpole had four separate printers in succession after Robinson. Finally in 1765 he engaged Thomas Kirgate, who remained in his service until Walpole's death in 1797.

Several of Walpole's own works were issued at Strawberry Hill, but not, strangely enough, his major literary work, *The Castle of Otranto*. The first work issued by the press was Thomas Gray's *Odes . . .* (1757). The genuine first edition of this work is printed on "thin" paper, that is, the regular paper used by the press. The edition on "thick" Dutch paper is now accepted as a reprint made by Thomas Kirgate in about 1790. (*See* Allen T. Hazen's *Bibliography of the Strawberry Hill Press*, New Haven, Yale University Press, 1942.) Very little printing was done at Strawberry Hill after 1789.

streamer   A printed horizontal poster or display piece of the kind often used for window advertising.

strip in   To combine one photographic negative with another or others, preparatory to using all in making a printing plate. In lithography the operation of stripping is analogous to the operation of imposing in letterpress.

struck-image   Synonym for direct-impression.

style sheet   (1) A guide to *house style* (*q.v.*). (2) A list of selected typefaces, sizes, arrangement of heads, etc., for a given publication.

subhead   A secondary heading or title, usually set in less prominent type than a main heading, to divide the entries under a subject.

subject heading   A word, or group of words, under which all material dealing with a given subject is entered in an index, catalog, or bibliography.

subroutine   In a computer program, a small routine which is part of a larger routine. *See also* routine.

subscription books   Editions of single books or sets, published for sale by subscription or by mail.

subscription library   A privately-owned library operated by and for the members, who pay annual dues.

subsidiary rights   Rights to a literary property other than that of original publication. *See also* rights.

subsidy publishing   (1) The publishing of works of specialized interest to a small group (e.g., a company or local history) or of scholarly works, generally not expected to be a commercial success, for which a grant or fund is provided by the author or by a foundation or other institution, to cover costs wholly or in part. A work so published may also be called a *sponsored book*, especially if the sponsoring organization or person has guaranteed to purchase a significant quantity of the edition. (2) Another designation for vanity publishing, in which a book is produced with little or no regard to the merit of the work at the author's expense and at no risk to the publisher. *See also* vanity publishers.

subtitle   An additional, or second title of a book. For example, "The Book: *The Story of Printing and Bookmaking*."

super   (1) A gauze-like fabric glued to the backbone of a book during the lining stage of binding for added strength. (2) Short for super-calendered. *See also* lining.

super-calendered   The glossiest finish that can be given to paper, short of coating it. *See also* calendering.

super royal octavo *See* book sizes.

superior figures Small numerals, thus *footnote*[2], used to indicate footnotes or in formulas.

supplement *See* appendix.

suppressed Withdrawn from public sale or circulation, either by the act of the publisher or bookseller, by group pressure, or by a court decision. *See* censor; censorship.

swash letters Italic capitals having top or bottom flourishes or both.

Sweynheym, Conrad and **Pannartz, Arnold** The first printers in Italy (fl. 1465–1473). They had migrated from Mainz, Germany, and headed for Rome with the intention of starting a press there. While resting at the Benedictine monastery at Subiaco, some sixty miles from Rome, they were invited to set up a printing establishment in the monastery itself. Between 1465 and 1467 they printed four books at Subiaco and then moved to Rome and set up their plant at the Massimi Palace. In 1473 they dissolved their partnership. During their joint career they produced twenty-nine separate works.

The type used in the printing of the Subiaco books combined the better qualities of the gothic and of the roman. In 1900 Emery Walker and Sydney Cockerell designed a type for C. H. St. John Hornby based upon the semi-gothic type used by Sweynheym and Pannartz, and named their design the Subiaco type. It was first used by Hornby in the Ashendene Press edition of Dante's *Inferno* (1902).

symbolic language Description of arithmetic and logic functions by means of symbols. Such symbolic language is used in the writing of computer programs.

system A collection of parts—men, machines, methods—organized to accept certain input and accomplish a specified objective. Although used widely to indicate computer installations and operations, the term is properly applied to virtually any organized activity or endeavor.

t.e.g. Abbreviation for *top edge gilt* (*q.v.*).

TOP Invoice symbol meaning "temporarily out of print."

TOS Invoice symbol meaning "temporarily out of stock."

table of contents A list of the divisions of a book, usually chapter headings or main subjects, arranged in the sequence in which they appear and constituting part of the *front matter* (*q.v.*) of the volume.

tail-piece A small ornament or illustration at the end of a chapter.

talking book A spoken rendition of a book, made available in recorded form, devised especially for the blind.

tall copy A book that stands a bit higher than others printed at the same time by reason of having been trimmed more sparingly. cf. large-paper edition.

tape Paper or magnetically coated plastic ribbon used to carry computer-coded data to and from various machines in a system or as storage of data in coded form.

tape merging The process of merging data from two or more tapes into a single set of data. *See also* merging.

tape reader A device for sensing data encoded on a tape and entering it in the computer. There are readers for magnetic tapes and readers for perforated paper tapes. *See also* magnetic storage; perforated tape; read; tape.

tapes Strips of cloth or tape pasted or sewed to the back of a book, the ends of which are glued or laced down to the cover to strengthen the binding.

tariff on books Obsolete. *See* Florence Agreement.

tear sheet Any page torn from a book or magazine, to be used as a sample, for checking, etc.

temporary storage An area of working storage not reserved for one use, but employed at different times during a computer run for various purposes.

text The main matter, as distinguished from the display matter, front matter, notes, appendix, and index.

text editing Synonym for editing.

text edition Some publishers provide both a trade edition and a text edition of certain books. The text edition, presumably for use in education, carries both a lower list price and a lower discount, with the expectation that it will be purchased in quantity.

textbook A book used for the study of a particular subject; a manual of instruction.

textile binding An ornate fabric style of binding. There was a fad for binding of this sort during the Renaissance in France and England. In England this "textile" style, as it is now known to collectors, retained its popularity into the eighteenth century, many books being sumptuously bound in colored satin and velvet, often embellished with beautiful needlework in many-colored silks, and with gold and silver threads.

thirty; 30   A term used mainly in newspaper offices, meaning "the end."

thirtytwomo (32mo)   *See* book sizes.

Thomas, Isaiah (1749–1831)   American printer-publisher-bookseller. When very young he was apprenticed as a printer to Zechariah Fowle in Boston, and worked as an apprentice in various parts of the colonies. In 1770 he formed a partnership with Fowle and established *The Massachusetts Spy*, issued thrice-weekly; shortly afterward, under his sole ownership, issued semi-weekly. In the spring of 1775 he moved his presses and types from Boston and set up in Worcester. Here he published and sold books, built a paper mill and bindery, and continued *The Spy*. He was the most noted printer of children's books of his time, and he reprinted, by arrangement, the charming juveniles of John Newbery of London, and his descendants.

Isaiah Thomas printed some 400 works, including his own *History of Printing in America* . . . (2 vols., 1810), a work described as important and thorough. In 1812 he founded the American Antiquarian Society, in Worcester; he endowed it with his fine library, and served as its first president.

three-color   *See* process color.

three-decker   A term applied to the three-volume novels as published in England in the latter half of the nineteenth century. Most of these novels, in cloth bindings, were offered for sale at 31 shillings 6 pence, and they were sold at substantial discount largely to circulating libraries. The format was abandoned in the late 1890s after an attack was made on the method of publishing by Sir Hall Caine, whose novel, *The Manxman*, was published in one volume in 1894, after the big circulating libraries had refused to handle the book.

three-quarter binding   *See* binding.

throughput   The net amount of production that can be put through the complete computerized typesetting system, as opposed to individual processing speeds of various components in the system. Throughput usually is limited by the slowest device in the system.

thumb index   An alphabetical or subject index cut into the front edges of a book to facilitate quick reference.

tie   In binding, narrow strips of leather, linen, or other material attached to the covers of a book to be tied across its fore-edges to prevent the curling of the binding. A feature especially of many vellum-bound books, old and new.

tight back   A book in which the back of the cover is glued directly to the spine of the book, rather than leaving it loose to bow outward as in a hollow-back book.

'til forbid   An instruction, usually in connection with a subscription, to treat as a standing order until notified to the contrary.

time-sharing   Use of a computer or other device for multiple purposes during the same time period. A time-sharing computer system enables many people to use the machine at the same time.

tint block   (1) A panel of color on which type or an illustration may be printed. (2) The plate used for printing the panel of color. A tint block may print the color solid or it may contain a screen or Benday so as to print a less-than-solid tint of the color.

tipping in   The operation of pasting into a book a separate leaf, an illustration, or a signature. Known also as *pasting in. See also* inserts.

tissue   In bookmaking, very thin papers, almost transparent, used to cover the face of an engraving or etched illustration to prevent setoff unto text pages.

title entry   A catalog or index entry filed under the title of a work.

title page   A page at the beginning of a book, usually on the right, giving its title, its author (if acknowledged), and usually its publisher, with place and date of publication. *See* front matter.

to-order book   Synonym for custom book.

tooling   Decoration on the binding of a book made by heated tools or stamps used to apply pigment or metal foil. *See also* blind tooling.

top edge gilt   A book in which only the top edges of the leaves have been gilt.

torn-tape system   A system in which perforated paper tape is produced by each of the various machines in the system and torn off at each machine's output device, after which the tape is manually carried to the next unit and mounted on a reader for input.

Tory, Geoffroy or **Geofroy** (1480?–1533)   French artist, engraver, typographer, and designer of letters, borders, and devices. His decorative illustrations and borders introduced what was to become the characteristic style of French Renaissance book decoration, and he was mainly responsible for the abandonment of the black-letter type in favor of the modern roman letter. He also introduced into French printing the accent, the apostrophe, and the cedilla. The results of his researches in the French language, his theories of geometrical letter design, etc., are set forth in his great work, *Champfleury*, published in 1529.

tracing   Information on a main entry catalog card, giving the other headings under which the work is listed.

track   The portion of a moving storage medium that is accessible to a single reading device.

trade binding   *See* binding.

trade books   Books intended for the general public, and marketed through bookstores and to libraries, as distinct from *textbooks, subscription books*, etc.

trade edition   An edition of a book intended for sale through bookstores to the general public or for general circulation in libraries, as distinct from an edition of the same book intended for some other use (e.g., textbook) or for sale through some other channel (e.g., subscription books).

trade publisher   A publisher of books intended primarily for sale through retail outlets or for general circulation by libraries.

trade list   Publisher's list of available titles, with list prices and discount categories. The trade lists of most U.S. publishers are collected annually into the multi-volume *Publishers' Trade List Annual*, published by the R. R. Bowker Company.

trans.; tr.   (1) In cataloging, an abbreviation for translated. (2) In proofreading, an abbreviation for transpose.

translation   Conversion of one language into another, either manually or automatically.

transmission   The sending of material from one point to another. *See also* data transmission.

transpose   In printing, to change or exchange the position of lines, words, or letters as shown in proof.

traveler   In the book industry, a salesman who visits prospective customers of the publisher (booksellers, librarians, university department heads, school authorities, wholesalers, purchasing agents) to show samples of or literature about the firm's forthcoming titles, and to obtain orders for them; also to transmit complaints, and assist in promotion and other areas.

tree calf   *See* mottled calf.

trimmed edges   One or more edges of a book trimmed by machinery, as opposed to *uncut edges (q.v.)*.

tubular back   A book with a tubular piece of fabric glued to the spine of the volume and to the back of the cover. This produces a book with the cover fastened to the book as in a tight-back binding, but also with a flexible back that can curve outward when the book is opened, as in a hollow-back book. *See also* hollow-back; tight back.

turned letter   Type placed upside down in composed matter to show that type of the right letter is not available and is to be supplied later. It shows in the proof as two black marks, thus: ▬

twelvemo (12mo)   *See* book sizes.

twentyfourmo (24mo)   *See* book sizes.

two up   Printing two of the same subject with one impression in any printing process. In letterpress, duplicate plates are used; in lithography, the plates bear two sets of printing images. For long runs of small items it is a saving of time and cost to print multiples at the same time, which may be two, four, eight, and even more up. Also applied to binding two or more copies at the same time.

tympan   Hard paper used to cover the platen or cylinder of a printing press to provide the correct support for the sheet being printed.

type   The basis of the Western invention of printing, originally signifying small, individually cast metal units bearing a face in relief that will produce a letter, figure, or other character; capable of assembling into text and usable in a printing press. The growth of nonmetallic composition suggests redefinition of type with emphasis on its visual properties; e.g., as a standardized design of letter forms, numerals, etc. following a common style.

typefaces   *See* name of face, or of its designer. A good showing of comparative examples is provided in the sample books of manufacturers and trade composition houses.

type-high   The height of type in the United States is .918 of an inch. Electros, engravings, and other plates which are to run with type must be blocked type-high. Unless there is type in the form, however, it is usual to make plates much thinner. The printer fastens them to a patent base which brings them up type-high. Type-high has lost all importance in photographic and electronic composition.

type page   The part of a page that contains the type, exclusive of the margins.

typescript   Typewritten material, as a manuscript.

typesetter   Compositor; one who sets type.

typewriter composition   Synonym for direct-impression composition.

typographer   Originally, a printer thoroughly familiar with all aspects of type and typesetting. At present, a designer highly skilled in the selection and arrangement of type. The typographer often specifies type images. Sometimes called *type director*.

typographical error (typo)   A mistake made by the typesetter.

typography   (1) The art of composing from movable type. (2) The arrangement and appearance of printed matter.

u & lc   Abbreviation for upper and lowercase. *See also* Proofreaders' Marks at end of book.

unauthorized edition   An edition issued without the consent of the author or the original publisher. The responsibility to the author is moral not legal. A *pirated edition* is an unauthorized reprint involving an infringement of copyright.

uncial   Pertaining to or consisting of a form of letter found in early Latin and Greek manuscripts. The uncial characters are large and of nearly uniform size, resembling modern capitals but with greater roundness. *See also* majuscule; minuscule.

uncut edges   Edges of a book untrimmed by machinery. Not to be confused with *unopened (q.v.)*.

underlay   In presswork, a piece of paper placed under the type form to bring it up to the proper height for printing. *See also* overlay.

underrun   Shortage in the number of copies printed.

union catalog   An author or a subject catalog listing the holdings of a group of libraries, generally established by a cooperative effort. The catalog may relate only to given subjects, or to entire collections.

Universal Copyright Convention   The major international copyright agreement, complete under UNESCO sponsorship in 1952, and since ratified by more than sixty nations. Under it, each signatory country extends to foreign works covered by U.C.C. the same protection which such country extends to works of its own nationals published within its own borders. (See *A Copyright Guide*, by Harriet F. Pilpel and Morton D. Goldberg. Bowker, 1969.) *See also* Berne Convention. At Paris in 1971, agreements amending both U.C.C. and Berne were reached, allowing developing countries to exercise international translation and reproduction rights (i.e., to issue "compulsory licenses" for such rights), in order to obtain adequate educational and cultural materials without prohibitive cost, while recognizing international copyright principles and avoiding piracy. The 1971 revision came into effect July 10, 1974, following adherence by the required twelve countries.

universal decimal classification (UDC)   A classification scheme issued under the auspices of the Federation Internationale de Documentation (FID). Originally based upon the Dewey Decimal Classification, but developed into a more detailed system to make it possible to class subjects very precisely. Not only books but also reports, patents, specifications, and articles in periodicals can be classed and indexed under the UDC scheme.

university press   A nonprofit publishing house attached to a university (or serving a group of universities and other scholarly institutions), and specializing in the publication of scholarly books.

unjustified tape   Encoded tape lacking any kind of coding to specify end-of-line breaks or hyphenations. *See also* idiot tape; raw tape.

unopened   An unopened book is one whose untrimmed edges have not been opened by hand, as with a paper knife.   Not to be confused with *uncut edges* (*q.v.*).

until forbid   *See* 'til forbid.

Unwin, Sir Stanley (1884–1968)   British and international book industry leader; head of a distinguished house, George Allen & Unwin, Ltd.; twice president of the International Publishers' Association, and a fighter for the strengthening of international copyright. His *The Truth About Publishing* (Bowker) is a spicy, authoritative, still standard work about the procedures of book publishing.

Updike, Daniel Berkeley (1860–1941)   American printer and publisher. Founded the Merrymount Press, Boston (1893), for which Bertram G. Goodhue designed his Merrymount type. Updike was an author and printing historian as well as a printer, and he had a strong influence on the development of typography in America. His *Printing Types: their History, Forms and Use* (2 vols., 1922), is still a standard text. He was gifted in liturgical printing; the first work of his press was *The Altar Book . . . Use of the American Church* (1896), and one of his finest works was the 1931 edition of *The Book of Common Prayer*.

uppercase   The capital letters in any font of type. So called because, in hand-set type, they were usually kept in the tray above the small or lowercase letters. *See also* case.

v.d.   Cataloging abbreviation for "various dates."

VDT   Abbreviation for video display terminal.

VET   Abbreviation for video editing terminal.

VLT   Abbreviation for video layout terminal.

v.p.   Abreviation for "various places" or "various publishers."

v.y.   Abbreviation for "various years."

Van Gelder paper   A brand of fine paper produced in Holland. Famous for a hundred years or more. Used principally for fine editions and also, in an antique finish, by artists for drawings, watercolors, and sketches.

vandyke   A type of *blueprint* (*q.v.*). *See also* proofs.

vanity publishers   A trade designation for publishing concerns that specialize in producing books not at their own risk, but at the author's risk and expense. They sign publishing contracts with inexperienced authors by appealing to their desire to see their writings in print at whatever cost. Sometimes called subsidy or cooperative publishers. *See also* subsidy publishing.

variant   A book that differs in one or more features from others of the same impression. Variations may occur in the sheets, binding, etc., or in two or more of these. There may be, and sometimes are, two or more variants within a single impression. These variations are of such nature that positive sequence of printing or stamping cannot be established. If sequence is known or discovered *states* and *issues* (*qq.v.*) are established.

variorum   Abbreviated from the Latin "cum notis variorum," with notes of various persons. Applied to a publication containing notes by various editors; e.g., a *variorum* edition of Shakespeare's works.

varnishing   Coating frequently applied to book jackets to give them a glossy appearance. Varnish in its liquid state is like printing ink, and is applied on a printing press. *See also* laminated.

vellum   The skin of a calf, *unsplit* and specially treated for use in writing or printing on, or for the binding of books. It is a finer material than parchment (*q.v.*), although at one time the word parchment was used to mean both parchment and vellum. Most medieval manuscripts were written on vellum, and a few copies of various editions during the first seventy-five years of printing were also printed on vellum. The finest vellum, known as *uterine vellum*, was made in the thirteenth and fourteenth centuries from the skins of unborn or stillborn animals, and it was used only for the most expensive manuscripts.

verbatim et literatim   Latin phrase meaning "word for word, letter for letter"; literally, a faithful translation or transcription.

verso   *See* recto.

vertical file   A collection of pamphlets, clippings, and other nonbook materials, arranged vertically (upright) in filing drawers for ready reference.

video display terminal   A computer input-output device containing a cathode-ray display tube and a typewriter-like keyboard. The material to be worked on is displayed on the tube face, and changes are made in this material via the keyboard. The displayed material changes as the changes are keyed in by the operator. *See also* video editing terminal; video layout terminal.

video display tube   Synonym for cathode-ray tube.

video editing terminal   A video display terminal specifically designed for performing editing functions on text matter. *See also* editing; video display terminal.

video layout terminal   A video display terminal specifically designed for sizing and positioning type in a graphic arrangement, or a terminal which permits the operator to prepare a diagrammatic representation on the screen to guide placement of the actual type by the computer and phototypesetter. *See also* page map; video display terminal.

vignette   (1) A small decorative design placed on a title page or at the head or tail of a chapter. (2) An illustration having a background that is shaded gradually away.

voice-grade service   A class of telephone-line service that can carry voice traffic or data at speeds up to 2,400 bits per second.

Vulgate   The Latin Bible authorized by the Roman Catholic Church. Translated by St. Jerome in the fourth century.

W   Invoice symbol meaning "will advise in a few days."

w.a.f.   With all faults. An abbreviation used in catalogs to signify that the item is or may be defective and is sold *as is* with no return privileges.

wf   In proof corrections, "wf" means that a letter (or letters) from a wrong *font* of type has been used.

Walker, Sir Emery (1851–1933)   Engraver and printer, a forceful spirit in the fine-printing movement of the late nineteenth century in England. After his lecture on types and printing given at the Arts and Crafts Exhibition of 1888, William Morris suggested that they should design a new type together. Walker agreed, and this brought about the founding of the Kelmscott Press (*q.v.*) by Morris. In 1900 Walker formed a partnership with T. J. Cobden-Sanderson and founded the Doves Press. The partnership was dissolved by Cobden-Sanderson in 1908. A brief summary of their association is given in this Glossary under *Doves Press.* Walker was knighted in 1930.

want list   *See* desiderata.

wash drawing   A brushwork drawing usually made with diluted India ink or watercolor, so that, in addition to its blacks and whites, it contains gray tones.

washed   Badly foxed or soiled leaves can, during rebinding, be washed in javelle water or other preparation and put under a warm iron or press, after which they must usually be resized. A book so treated is sometimes identifiable by the odor of javelle water.

watermark   A design faintly showing in paper when held up to the light. This is made by the dandy roll on a Fourdrinier machine which presses down on the forming sheet just as the pulp is well drained and before the sheet begins to go through the series of drying rolls.

Paper for fine editions of books is frequently watermarked with a design to show that the paper was made specially for that edition.

waxing   The coating of photographic paper or reproduction proofs on the back side with a special wax which permits them to be adhered easily to a master sheet, yet also be removed and readhered readily. Used extensively in paste-up operations.

web press   *See* rotary press.

Webster, Noah (1758–1843)   American lexicographer, author, teacher, lawyer, etc. He was president of the Amherst Academy (1820–21) and helped found Amherst College. He was admitted to the bar at Hartford in 1781, and he did much work from 1782 to 1789 agitating for a uniform copyright law.

His first lexicographical publication, part one of *Grammatical Institute of the English Language* (1782–83), was a spelling book, later known as *Webster's Spelling Book* or *Blue-Backed Speller*. Parts II and III (1784–85) were a grammar and reader. The speller was used in all schools, and in the course of a century sold some sixty million copies. Webster's first real dictionary was the *Compendious Dictionary of the English Language* (1806). His fame rests on his more important work, *An American Dictionary of the English Language* (2 volumes, 1828).

weeding   Discarding books from a library collection.

Weems, Mason Locke (1759–1825)   American clergyman, book-agent, and writer, known as "Parson Weems," was born in Anne Arundel County, Md. After 1794 he served as traveling book salesman for Mathew Carey, Philadelphia publisher (*q.v.*), and sold books throughout the southern and middle states.

He wrote books and tracts on morality and temperance, and "biographies" (fictionized works) of notable Americans—Washington, General

Francis Marion, Franklin, and others. His *Life and Memorable Actions of George Washington* (1800) was first issued anonymously. The third edition (called the second on the newly worded title) was the first to bear Weems's name as author. In the fifth edition (1806) the hatchet and cherry tree story (invented by Weems) first appeared in book form.

Whatman, James (1741–1798)   One of the foremost English papermakers; his Turkey Mill dates back to 1693.

whiteprint   *See* blueprint.

Whittingham, Charles   *See* Chiswick Press.

wholesaler   One who buys from publishers and sells to retail booksellers or libraries. Also called *jobbers.*

wide   Any material, such as a chart or illustration, that is wider than the specified type page.

widow   A short single line at the top of a page or column, usually the last line of a paragraph. To be avoided in good typography.

window copy   Printed pages pasted up on sheets of paper with holes or windows cut in them so that both sides of each printed leaf are visible.

Wing, Donald Goddard   *See* Short-Title Catalogue.

wire-lines   In *laid paper* (*q.v.*), the closely spaced lines, as opposed to the *chain-lines* (*q.v.*).

wire marks   *See* wire-lines.

wire stitching   *See* stitching.

wired-program computer   A computer in which instructions and sequences for operations to be performed are permanently fixed by the interconnection of wires. *See also* stored-program computer.

Wise, Thomas James (1859–1937)   Book-collector, bibliographer, editor, and forger. Born at Gravesend, near London; employed at the age of sixteen as office boy by a firm dealing in essential oils; became an expert in the field and by the 1920s he was rich and retired.

At the age of eighteen he founded the Ashley Library by purchasing some of the lesser first editions of Shelley at low prices; by 1884, when he was twenty-five, he paid £45 for the Pisa edition (1821) of Shelley's *Adonais*; he became an active member of the Browning Society, and later, in 1886, of the Shelley Society; instigated "type-facsimile" reprints by both societies, many of the publications being under his editorship.

Between 1888 and 1899 Wise was the creator and promoter of sixty-some bogus first editions of works by Matthew Arnold, Elizabeth Barrett Browning, Robert Browning, Dickens, George Eliot, Kipling, William Morris, D. G. Rossetti, Ruskin, Stevenson, Swinburne, Tennyson, Thackeray, and others. A number of these were suspect long before they were exposed by John Carter and Graham Pollard in *An Enquiry Into the Nature of Certain Nineteenth Century Pamphlets* (London: Constable, 1934).

The most spectacular of the Wise forgeries is Elizabeth Barrett Browning's *Sonnets* . . . bearing the imprint: "Reading: Not for Publication. 1847." It was produced in 1893. The rarest of the forgeries (only three copies known) is Matthew Arnold's *Alaric at Rome* . . . which bears the imprint of the first edition, "Rugby: Combe and Crossley, 1840." This also was produced in 1893.

In addition to works edited by him, Wise produced many bibliographies, especially of Victorian authors. His magnum opus is the catalog of his own great library of English literature: *The Ashley Library . . . Printed Books, Manuscripts, and Autograph Letters* . . . (11 volumes, 1922–36). The library was purchased after his death by the British Museum, for £66,000.

The checking of the Ashley Library books at the British Museum brought to light at least thirty thefts by Wise of leaves from copies of seventeenth century English plays in the British Museum. Wise had stolen the leaves to "improve" or complete his own imperfect copies. The discovery was made by D. F. Foxon, a member of the Museum's staff, and his discoveries were published in an article in the *Times Literary Supplement* on 19 October 1956. The total of Wise's depredations was raised in number during the next three years, and Mr. Foxon gives a more complete census in his monograph, *Thomas J. Wise and the Pre-Restoration Drama*, published by the Bibliographical Society in 1959.

wood pulp   Paper pulp prepared from trees of various kinds. There are two distinct classes: (1) mechanical wood pulp or groundwood from which newsprint-type papers are made; (2) chemical pulp produced by various methods, as the sulfite, soda, and sulfate processes. *See also* chemical pulp.

woodcut; wood engraving   Illustrations or designs printed from inked wood blocks; or the blocks themselves. The design is drawn directly on the surface of the block and the parts which are not to print are cut away. The woodcut is cut with a knife along the grain of the plank; the wood engraving is engraved with a burin or graver across the grain on the cross section of the block.

The first dated woodcut (1418) is the picture of the "Brussels Virgin"; the earliest wood engraving was made by Thomas Bewick (1752–1828) generally considered to be its inventor. He also introduced the "white line" in which the design is in the white spaces rather than in the black lines. If many impressions from woodcut or wood engraving are needed, an electrotype is now usually made.

With the coming of photography, the design was transferred onto the wood block by photomechanics rather than by hand. This developed a craft of wood engraving rather distinct from the artist's. The camera, however, soon supplanted that process with the halftone (*q.v.*); woodcut and wood engraving are today used only in the making of artist's prints and, at times, in the illustration of limited edition books.

wooden boards Prior to the times of Aldus of Venice in the fifteenth century and for some time afterwards, the covers of bound books were made of thick wood over which the leather was stretched. Even small books had stiff covers a quarter of an inch thick and often beveled to a sharp edge to disguise this disproportionate thickness.

The use of pasteboard for bookbinding was not introduced until the end of the fifteenth century and at first was only employed upon books of small size.

word A set of characters which occupies a single storage location in a computer memory, and is handled as a unit in the machine.

Worde, Wynkyn de (d. 1535) Native of Lorraine, served as an assistant at William Caxton's press at Bruges; followed him to England in 1476 and served as foreman at the Westminster press. He succeeded to the press on Caxton's death in 1491. In 1500 he left Westminster and moved to Fleet Street in London; after 1509 he sold his books from his own shop in St. Paul's Churchyard. Between 1491 and 1535 he produced some 800 books, most of them undated.

work and turn Normally, one side of a sheet is printed from one form of type, the other side from a second form. But if the type for both sides can be fitted on a single form, it may become economical to print by the "work and turn" method whereby all the type for both sides of the finished job is printed on one side of a double-size sheet. The sheets are then turned over, left for right, and backed up from the same form. The pile of double-size sheets is then cut down the center yielding two piles, each properly printed on both sides. Running "work and turn" saves half the impressions that would be required for running the same job *sheetwise* (*q.v.*).

wove paper Paper that shows no pattern of the sort that distinguishes *laid paper* (*q.v.*).

woven materials *See* book cloth; nonwoven materials.

wrappers The printed or unprinted cover of a pamphlet or book bound in paper. Not to be confused with *boards* (*q.v.*) which, contemporaneously, means paper-covered binder's boards. Specifically wrappers, while often of the same stock as the body of the publication, are not part of the printed sheets comprising the publication. Rather they are separately affixed to the body of the publication by the binder. Some authorities, notably Will Ransom, prefer "wrapper" to "wrappers," the argument being that the object is singular and not plural. *See also* self-wrapper; jacket.

write   In a computer, to transcribe data on an output medium or to transfer data into a section of memory.

writers' conference   A seminar, usually held at colleges in the summer, attended by both established writers and students of writing, featuring lectures, workshops, and discussions conducted by specialists in their fields.

wrong font   *See* wf.

wrong-reading   A film image which reads from right to left and top to bottom when the emulsion surface of the film is facing the viewer.

XR   Abbreviation for "no returns permitted."

xerography   An electrostatic printing process which uses dry resin powder and heat to fuse images onto any kind of paper, as opposed to other types of electrostatic printing which use toners in solution to create images on special papers. Xerography is widely used as a photocopying process marketed under the trade name Xerox. *See* electrostatics.

xylography   Printing from blocks of wood, especially of an early or primitive kind. Such books are sometimes also called *xylographic books*, or *xylographica*. *See also* block books.

yapp   *See* divinity circuit.

yellow-back   The name given to the cheap editions popular in railway book stalls in the mid-nineteenth century. They were usually works of fiction bound in yellow covers.

young adult book   Designation for a book intended for adult circulation, but deemed suitable reading for young people from ninth through twelfth grades. A decision customarily based on recommendations of library periodicals or library organizations.

Zamorano, Agustin Vicente (1798–1842)   Pioneer printer of California, and executive secretary of California under the Mexican regime. Born at St. Augustine, Florida; received his schooling and grew to manhood in Mexico. By establishing the "farthest west" printing press of the United States in 1834 at Monterey, he became best known to history as the first printer in California. Twenty-one of his imprints are known, in addition to letterheads and stamped paper headings. Eleven of his imprints were broadsides or folders on official matters; six were of a miscellaneous nature, and four were books. The private book club in Los Angeles, the Zamorano Club, was named for him.

zinc etching   *See* line cut.

zinco   Abbreviation for zincograph, an etching on zinc used in letterpress; a rarely used term.

A SELECTED READING LIST

THE ART AND HISTORY OF THE BOOK

Aldis, Harry Gidney. *The Printed Book*. Rev. ed. by John Carter and E. S. Crutchley. Cambridge University Press, 1951. o.p.

Berry, W. Turner, and H. Edmund Poole. *Annals of Printing: A Chronological Encyclopaedia from Earliest Times to 1950*. University of Toronto Press, 1967. $16.50.

Clair, Colin. *A Chronology of Printing*. Praeger, 1969. $12.50.

Diringer, David. *The Hand-produced Book*. Philosophical Library, 1953. o.p.

Glaister, Geoffrey. *An Encyclopedia of the Book*. World, 1960. o.p.

Greenhood, David, and Helen Gentry. *Chronology of Books and Printing*, rev. ed. Macmillan, 1936. o.p.

Kenyon, Frederic G. *Books and Readers in Ancient Greece and Rome*. West, reprint of 1951 ed. 1973. $10.00.

McMurtrie, Douglas C. *The Book*: *The Story of Printing and Bookmaking*, 3rd rev. ed. Oxford University Press, 1943. $17.50.

Oswald, John Clyde. *A History of Printing*: *Its Development during Five Hundred Years*. Library Press, 1928. o.p.

Ransom, Will. *Private Presses and Their Books*. Bowker, 1929. o.p.

Vervliet, Hendrik D. L., ed. *The Book*: *Through Five Thousand Years*. Phaidon, 1972. $60.00.

Wroth, Lawrence C., ed. *A History of the Printed Book*; being Number Three of *The Dolphin*. Limited Editions Club, 1938. o.p.

BIBLIOGRAPHY AND BOOK COLLECTING

Bowers, Fredson T. *Principles of Bibliographical Description*. Princeton University Press, 1949; reprinted, Russell & Russell, 1962. $20.00.

Carter, John. *ABC for Book Collectors*. 5th ed. Knopf, 1973. $5.95.

Carter, John. *Books and Book-Collectors*. Dufour, 1957. $5.95.

Gaskell, Philip. *A New Introduction to Bibliography*. Oxford University Press, 1972. $9.50.

McKerrow, Ronald B. *An Introduction to Bibliography for Literary Students.* Oxford University Press, 1927. $12.75.

Winterich, John T., and David A. Randall. *A Primer of Book Collecting.* Crown, 1966. $5.95.

COPYRIGHT

Bogsch, Arpad. *The Law of Copyright under the Universal Convention.* 3d ed. Bowker, 1969. $32.50.

Kent, Allen, ed. *Copyright: Current Viewpoints on History, Laws, Legislation.* Bowker, 1972. $12.50.

Nicholson, Margaret. *Manual of Copyright Practice for Writers, Publishers, and Agents.* 2d ed. Oxford University Press, 1956. $7.50.

Pilpel, Harriet F., and Morton D. Goldberg. *A Copyright Guide.* 4th ed. Bowker, 1969. $5.50.

Rogers, Joseph W. *U.S. National Bibliography and the Copyright Law: An Historical Study.* Bowker, 1960. $5.25.

EDITORIAL

Bernstein, Theodore. *The Careful Writer.* Atheneum, 1965. $10.00.

Gross, Gerald, comp. *Editors on Editing.* Grosset & Dunlap, 1962. $2.65.

Manual of Style. 12th ed. University of Chicago Press, 1969. $10.00.

Skillin, Marjorie E., and Robert M. Gay. *Words Into Type.* Appleton, 1964. $7.90.

Strunk, William, Jr., and E. B. White. *Elements of Style.* 2d ed. Macmillan, 1972. $3.50; paper. $1.25.

PAPER, PRINTING, AND PRODUCTION

Bland, David. *A History of Book Illustration: The Illuminated Manuscript and the Printed Book.* 2nd rev. ed. University of California Press, 1969. $28.75.

Comparato, Frank E. *Books for the Millions: A History of the Men whose Methods and Machines Packaged the Printed Word.* Stackpole, 1971. $12.50.

Diehl, Edith. *Bookbinding: Its Background and Technique.* Kennikat, 1947. $27.50.

Grannis, Chandler, ed. *The Heritage of the Graphic Arts.* Bowker, 1972. $18.75.

Hunter, Dard. *Papermaking: The History and Technique of an Ancient Craft.* 2d ed. Knopf, 1947. $20.00.

Lee, Marshall. *Bookmaking: The Illustrated Guide to Design and Production.* Bowker, 1965. $15.95.

Melcher, Daniel, and Nancy Larrick. *Printing and Promotion Handbook; How to Plan, Produce, and Use Printing, Advertising and Direct Mail.* 3rd. ed. McGraw-Hill, 1966. $15.95.

Penrose Annual, edited by Herbert Spencer. Hastings House, 1973. $22.50.

Simon, Oliver. *Introduction to Typography.* Transatlantic Arts, 1949. $7.50.

Strauss, Victor. *The Printing Industry: An Introduction to Its Many Branches, Processes and Products.* Bowker, 1967. $29.75.

Updike, Daniel Berkeley. *Printing Types: Their History, Forms and Use.* 3d ed. Harvard University Press, 1962, 2 vols. $18.00.

PUBLISHING AND THE BOOK TRADE

Bailey, Herbert S., Jr. *The Art and Science of Book Publishing.* Harper, 1970. $7.95.

Bingley, Clive. *The Business of Book Publishing.* Pergamon, 1972. $9.50.

The Bowker Annual of Library and Book Trade Information. Bowker, 1974.

Cheney, O. H. *Economic Survey of the Book Industry.* Bowker, 1931. Reprinted 1960 with introduction by Robert Frase. o.p.

Dessauer, John P. *Book Publishing: What It Is, What It Does.* Bowker, 1974.

Grannis, Chandler B., ed. *What Happens in Book Publishing.* 2d ed., Columbia University Press, 1967. $10.00.

Gross, Sydney, and Phyllis B. Steckler, eds. *How to Run a Paperback Bookshop.* Bowker, 1963. $8.50.

Hackett, Alice Payne. *Seventy Years of Best Sellers: 1895–1965.* Bowker, 1967. $9.95.

Kerr, Chester. *A Report on American University Presses.* University of Oklahoma Press, 1949. $.50.

Lehmann-Haupt, Hellmut, Lawrence C. Roth, and Rollo G. Silver. *The Book in America.* rev. ed. Bowker, 1951. $16.75.

Mott, Frank Luther. *Golden Multitudes: A Study of Best Sellers, 1662–1945.* Bowker, 1960. $10.95.

Mumby, Frank A., and Ian Norrie. *Publishing and Bookselling: A History from Earliest Times to the Present Day.* 5th ed. Bowker, 1974. $33.50.

Nemeyer, Carol A. *Scholarly Reprint Publishing in the United States.* Bowker, 1972. $13.50.

Schick, Frank L. *The Paperbound Book in America: The History of Paperbacks and Their European Background.* Bowker, 1958. o.p.

Tebbel, John. *A History of Book Publishing in the United States.* 3 vols. Vol. 1: *The Creation of an Industry, 1640–1865.* Vol. 2: *The Expansion of an Industry, 1865–1919.* Bowker, 1972, 1975. $29.95 per vol.

Unwin, Sir Stanley. *The Truth about Publishing.* 7th rev. ed. Bowker, 1960. $3.25.

Proofreader's Marks

The symbols shown here are revised to accord with the *American National Standard Proof Corrections*, Z39.22-1974. Copyright by the American National Standards Institute, 1974.

Marginal Mark	Instruction	Mark in Text	Corrected Text
	Delete	Morison	Morison
	Delete and close up	bibbliography	bibliography
	Insert additional material in margin	Nicolas	Nicholas
stet	Retain crossed out material	Edwin and Robert Grabhorn	Edwin and Robert Grabhorn
✕	Broken type	bookseller	bookseller
	Straighten line	a foolish consistency is	a foolish consistency is
‖	Align vertically	Caslon Bodoni Janson	Caslon Bodoni Janson
¶	Start new paragraph	in 1474. In the next few years	in 1474. In the next few years
no ¶	Run on. No new paragraph	engraver and printer. He was one of	engraver and printer. He was one of
tr	Transpose words or letters indicated	Let not me to the marriage	Let me not to the marriage
	Invert letter indicated*	editor	editor
	Close up. No space	horn book	hornbook
lig	Use ligature	an ever-fixed mark	an ever-fixed mark
#	Insert space	bookclub	book club
	Push down space to avoid printing*	A famous printer	A famous printer
▱	Insert en quad	1.The first item	1. The first item
▭	Indent one em	Hickory	Hickory
	Indent two ems	Dickory	Dickory
	Indent three ems	Dock	Dock
⊐⊏	Center	Tick-Tock	Tick-Tock
⊐	Move to the right	mountain peak,	mountain peak,
⊏	Move to the left	From the snow	From the snow
⊔	Lower to proper position	true minds	true minds
⊓	Raise to proper position	admit impediment	admit impediment
?	Is this correct?	not impossible	not possible
caps	Capitals	william shakespeare	William Shakespeare
lc	Lower case	Havre De Grace	Havre de Grace
sc	Small capitals	Berne Convention	BERNE CONVENTION
c & sc	Capitals and small capitals	Berne Convention	BERNE CONVENTION

Marginal Mark	Instruction	Mark in Text	Corrected Text
rom	Roman	*first* printing	first printing
ital	Italic	in the Times	in the *Times*
bf	Bold face	Extra	**Extra**
bf ital	Bold face italic	Illustrations	***Illustrations***
∧	Insert comma	composition␐printing and binding	composition, printing and binding
;/	Insert semicolon	given␐it is also	given; it is also
:/	Insert colon	divided as follows␐	divided as follows:
⊙	Insert period	in all fields␐	in all fields.
?/	Insert question mark	to a summer's day␐	to a summer's day?
!/!	Insert exclamation point	Hark␐Hark␐the lark	Hark! Hark! the lark
/=/	Insert hyphen	book␐hunter	book-hunter
∨	Insert apostrophe	at Heavens␐gate	at Heaven's gate
∨∨ ∨∨	Insert quotation marks	␐Yes,␐quoth I.	"Yes," quoth I.
∨2∨	Insert superior character	in his latest book␐	in his latest book^2
∧2∧	Insert inferior character	H␐2O	H_2O
(/)	Insert parentheses	text␐see page 5␐	text (see page 5)
[/]	Insert brackets	n. d.␐1850␐	n. d. [1850]
1/N	Insert one en dash	1900␐1950	1900–1950
1/M	Insert one em dash	editor␐the person in charge of	editor—the person in charge of
wf	Wrong font*	upoⓃme proved	upon me proved
eg #	Space evenly	nor✓no✓man✓ever loved	nor no man ever loved
hr #	Hair space	ANNO DOMINI	ANNO DOMINI
(sp)	Spell out	④score and⑦years	Four score and seven years
ld	Insert lead	If this be error and Then I never writ	If this be error and Then I never writ
(out–see copy)	There is an omission here. See copy	our forefathers␐a new nation	our forefathers set forth upon this continent a new nation
tr	Transfer to position shown by caret	(proposition) conceived in liberty and dedicated to the ∧	conceived in liberty and dedicated to the proposition

*These three symbols (⌒, ⌊ , *wf*) are unlikely to be needed in marking photocomposed text.